PRAISE FOR CustomerCulture

"Mike Basch was a key member of the early FedEx team that instilled the extreme dedication to customer service that revolutionized the transportation industry."

Frederick W. Smith
Founder and CEO, FedEx, Memphis, TN

"Creating raving fan customers is the only way to go. Michael Basch, in his book, *CustomerCulture*, will teach you how to do that every day!"

Ken Blanchard
coauthor, "The One Minute Manager®" and "Whale Done!™"

"Basch has captured in *CustomerCulture* the causal factors as to why certain organizations excel in customer loyalty while others continually struggle to keep their customer first."

Jim Barksdale
former CEO of Netscape and
current partner of The Barksdale Group, Menlo Park, CA

"*CustomerCulture* clearly and succinctly points the way to the magical land of customer service excellence with enlightening insights into applications for businesses large and small. Buy it, read it, do it; make your world a better place."

Roger Frock
former General Manager, FedEx, Memphis, TN

"Mike Basch knows so many ways to get your organization closely bonded with your customers, members, or clients that it would be a business shame for you not to read this book at least three times and then make it mandatory reading by every manager, supervisor, staff member, and new hire. I've learned more about creating world class business culture and owning the relationship with your customers from Mike Basch than I have from any other expert on the subject.
Pray you read this book before your competition does."

Jay Abraham
Author of "Getting Everything You Can Out of All You've Got"

"There's more wisdom in this book than you would gain as a graduate from a Top 5 business school! There's nothing like having 'been there and done that' and Mike Basch has done both! That's what you will learn from this reading this book, authored by a true 'Captain of Industry.' Mike is both the message and the messenger when it comes to connecting your customers and your 'Corporate Culture.' The end results? A healthier bottom line! You're in the people business! It's the customer, Stupid!"

Francis X. Maguire
President/CEO, Hearth Communications, Los Angeles, CA

"I had the good fortune to work with Mike Basch for a number of years. His understanding of the importance of organizational culture and his ability to build or transform cultures delivers ever-increasing value to customers, employees, and owners. If you want to take your culture to the next level, implement the principles in *CustomerCulture*."

Dennis Jones
COO, Commerce One, Pleasanton, CA

"Mike Basch's work with Larson-Juhl's managers helped us to understand the relationship between our actions, the company culture, and its impact on the people who actually build (or destroy) customer loyalty—our frontline team members. His *CustomerCulture* thinking got us to implement real goals, measurements, and rewards—all of which led to passionate employees delivering extraordinary service. I grew as a leader in the process."

Bill Trimarco
Senior Vice President, Larson-Juhl, Norcross, GA

"An organization of people is a living, breathing organism. Its soul is the cultural structures that give the organization its character, its purpose, and thus, its value to its customers. Mike Basch's *Customer-Culture* shows us as leaders in business how to proactively build those structures that breathe life into our organization. It's a great book!"

Thomas Oliver
Chairman & CEO, Six Continents Hotels, PLC, London, England

"You have in your hands a phenomenal 'toolkit' for unlocking the full potential of your organization. Mike Basch has been in the trenches and knows how to make these tools work in the real world. His techniques are incredibly simple and incredibly powerful. I use them daily, both with my clients, in my own company, and now in a university program I teach for executives who are leading organizational change. This book is the core of that program because it's about putting theory into action for enduring results."

Ravi Tangri
CEO, Chrysalis Performance Strategies Inc., Halifax, N.S., Canada

"Now the other 95% of companies have access to the roadmap responsible for making the top 5% of companies so great. It begins with a positive culture."

Scott de Moulin
President/Founder, Destiny Training Systems, Los Angeles, CA

Customer Culture:
How FedEx® and Other Great Companies Put the Customer First Every Day

Customer Culture:
How FedEx® and Other Great Companies Put the Customer First Every Day

Michael D. Basch

Prentice Hall
FINANCIAL TIMES

An Imprint of PEARSON EDUCATION
Upper Saddle River, NJ • New York • London • San Francisco • Toronto • Sydney
Tokyo • Singapore • Hong Kong • Cape Town • Madrid
Paris • Milan • Munich • Amsterdam

www.ft-ph.com

Library of Congress Cataloging-in-Publication Data

Editorial/production supervision: *Laura Burgess*
Executive editor: *Tim Moore*
Editorial assistant: *Allyson Kloss*
Marketing Manager: *Bryan Gambrel*
Manufacturing buyer: *Maura Zaldivar*
Cover design director: *Jerry Votta*
Cover design: *Anthony Gemmellaro*
Art Director: *Gail Cocker-Bogusz*

 © 2003 by Prentice Hall PTR
A division of Pearson Education, Inc.
Upper Saddle River, New Jersey 07458

ISBN 0-13-130320-1

Pearson Education LTD.
Pearson Education Australia PTY, Limited
Pearson Education Singapore, Pte. Ltd.
Pearson Education North Asia Ltd.
Pearson Education Canada, Ltd.
Pearson Educación de Mexico, S.A. de C.V.
Pearson Education—Japan
Pearson Education Malaysia, Pte. Ltd.

FINANCIAL TIMES PRENTICE HALL BOOKS

For more information, please go to www.ft-ph.com

Dr. Judith M. Bardwick, PhD
  Seeking the Calm in the Storm: Managing Chaos in Your Business Life

Thomas L. Barton, William G. Shenkir, and Paul L. Walker
  Making Enterprise Risk Management Pay Off:
  How Leading Companies Implement Risk Management

Michael Basch
  CustomerCulture: How FedEx and Other Great Companies Put the
  Customer First Every Day

Deirdre Breakenridge
  Cyberbranding: Brand Building in the Digital Economy

William C. Byham, Audrey B. Smith, and Matthew J. Paese
  Grow Your Own Leaders: How to Identify, Develop, and Retain
  Leadership Talent

Jonathan Cagan and Craig M. Vogel
  Creating Breakthrough Products: Innovation from Product Planning
  to Program Approval

Subir Chowdhury
  The Talent Era: Achieving a High Return on Talent

Sherry Cooper
  Ride the Wave: Taking Control in a Turbulent Financial Age

James W. Cortada
  21st Century Business: Managing and Working
  in the New Digital Economy

James W. Cortada
  Making the Information Society: Experience, Consequences,
  and Possibilities

Aswath Damodaran
  The Dark Side of Valuation: Valuing Old Tech, New Tech,
  and New Economy Companies

Henry A. Davis and William W. Sihler
  Financial Turnarounds: Preserving Enterprise Value

Sarv Devaraj and Rajiv Kohli
  The IT Payoff: Measuring the Business Value
  of Information Technology Investments

Jaime Ellertson and Charles W. Ogilvie
Frontiers of Financial Services: Turning Customer Interactions Into Profits

Nicholas D. Evans
Business Agility: Strategies for Gaining Competitive Advantage through Mobile Business Solutions

Kenneth R. Ferris and Barbara S. Pécherot Petitt
Valuation: Avoiding the Winner's Curse

David Gladstone and Laura Gladstone
Venture Capital Handbook: An Entrepreneur's Guide to Raising Venture Capital, Revised and Updated

David R. Henderson
The Joy of Freedom: An Economist's Odyssey

Philip Jenks and Stephen Eckett, Editors
The Global-Investor Book of Investing Rules: Invaluable Advice from 150 Master Investors

Thomas Kern, Mary Cecelia Lacity, and Leslie P. Willcocks
Netsourcing: Renting Business Applications and Services Over a Network

Al Lieberman, with Patricia Esgate
The Entertainment Marketing Revolution: Bringing the Moguls, the Media, and the Magic to the World

Frederick C. Militello, Jr., and Michael D. Schwalberg
Leverage Competencies: What Financial Executives Need to Lead

D. Quinn Mills
Buy, Lie, and Sell High: How Investors Lost Out on Enron and the Internet Bubble

Dale Neef
E-procurement: From Strategy to Implementation

John R. Nofsinger
Investment Blunders (of the Rich and Famous)…And What You Can Learn From Them

John R. Nofsinger
Investment Madness: How Psychology Affects Your Investing… And What to Do About It

Tom Osenton
Customer Share Marketing: How the World's Great Marketers Unlock Profits from Customer Loyalty

W. Alan Randolph and Barry Z. Posner
Checkered Flag Projects: 10 Rules for Creating and Managing Projects that Win, Second Edition

Stephen P. Robbins
The Truth About Managing People...And Nothing but the Truth

Eric G. Stephan and Wayne R. Pace
Powerful Leadership: How to Unleash the Potential in Others and Simplify Your Own Life

Jonathan Wight
Saving Adam Smith: A Tale of Wealth, Transformation, and Virtue

Yoram J. Wind and Vijay Mahajan, with Robert Gunther
Convergence Marketing: Strategies for Reaching the New Hybrid Consumer

About *Customer Culture*

"Basch has captured in Customer Culture the causal factors as to why certain organizations excel in customer loyalty while others continually struggle to keep their customer first."

—Jim Barksdale, former CEO of Netscape,
and current partner of the Barksdale Group

Customers. By now, you know how important they are. So do your competitors. But most companies simply haven't delivered on the promise of customer focus. That gives you an immense opportunity—if only you can grab it. CustomerCulture shows you how.

Author Michael D. Basch created the legendary sales and service organization of FedEx, founded its Business Logistics Division, and built its $100 million SuperHub. Since then, companies worldwide have called upon his unparalleled insight into customer service. Now, he's distilled that insight into a hands-on roadmap for every company, regardless of size or industry.

No more lectures. No more "happy talk." No more mission statements. This is a detailed, start-to-finish plan for building a customer-centric culture—and systems that let good people deliver outstanding service.

Talk won't do the job—it will take hard work and the specific techniques, solutions, and insights you'll find in only one place: CustomerCulture.

Good people + great systems = extraordinary results
Why great systems are your #1 customer differentiator—and how to build them

Real examples, real solutions, real life
Specific case studies and techniques from one of the world's leading customer service experts

The six elements of a winning customer culture
Vision, values, goals, relevance, feedback, and actions

Inculcating and strengthening a customer-centric business culture
Beyond meaningless "happy talk" and mission statements

Why customer systems fail, and how to fix them
Identifying systemic causes, ensuring goal clarity, and maximizing feedback

Moving your business up the value curve
Meeting customer needs that transcend "mere" products and services

This book is dedicated to
my wife and partner, Karen, and to
my three children Lisa, Jeff, and Michael

About the Author

 MICHAEL D. BASCH was a founding officer of FedEx, where he spent 10 years as Senior Vice President. He was part of the explosively creative management team that took FedEx from 0 to $1 billion, as it built a company cited by Fortune as one of the decade's most well-managed companies. Basch led the teams that invented the bar code tracing system at FedEx, built its SuperHub, and founded the FedEx Business Logistics Division.

Before joining FedEx, Basch spent eight years with UPS in Sales, Personnel, Operations, and Industrial Engineering. After leaving FedEx, he founded and served as President of Service Impact, a firm specializing in advancing the art, science, and practice of leadership.

He is currently Chief Information Officer of Enalasys Corporation, a company based in Calexico, CA, that develops advanced diagnostic technology to improve the quality, comfort, and cost of the indoor environment.

CONTENTS

FOREWORD XVII

INTRODUCTION XXI

PART 1   THE THEORY 1

CHAPTER 1   AMERICA, YOU HAVE A NEW AIRLINE
AND...A NEW STANDARD OF SERVICE 3

CHAPTER 2   SYSTEMS DRIVE PEOPLE 21

A UPS SYSTEMS EXAMPLE: REDUCING
TRANSACTION COSTS... 28
BACKGROUND 28
PROBLEM 29
SYSTEMIC CAUSE 30
SOLUTION 30
RESULT 31
POSTSCRIPT 31

ANOTHER UPS EXAMPLE: AN ELEGANT SOLUTION
TO REDUCE MIS-SORTS 32
BACKGROUND 32
PROBLEM 33
SYSTEMIC CAUSE 33
SOLUTION 34
RESULT 36
POSTSCRIPT 36

A FEDERAL EXPRESS EXAMPLE: ON-TIME
DEPARTURE 36
BACKGROUND 36

PROBLEM 37

SYSTEMIC CAUSE 37

RESULTS 38

POSTSCRIPT 38

CHAPTER 3 VISION 41

THE FIRST NEED OF PEOPLE IS TO HAVE THEIR
PHYSICAL NEEDS MET 43

STAGE TWO IS MEETING INFORMATIONAL NEEDS
45

STAGE THREE IS MEETING EMOTIONAL NEEDS 47

STAGE FOUR IS SPIRITUAL NEEDS 50

CHAPTER 4 VALUES AS WORDS VERSUS VALUES AS
ACTIONS 53

CHAPTER 5 GOALS 63

CHAPTER 6 RELEVANCE 73

YOU GET WHAT YOU RECOGNIZE 83

INVENTION OF THE EAGLE CARD 85

LEGENDARY STORIES ENCOURAGE LEGENDARY
BEHAVIORS 88

CHAPTER 7 YOU CAN'T MANAGE OR INNOVATE WHAT
YOU CAN'T MEASURE 95

A GOOD EXAMPLE WHERE FEEDBACK HAS BEEN
LOST IS THE U.S. HEALTHCARE SYSTEM 103

CHAPTER 8 EXTRAORDINARY SERVICE IS DELIVERED
BY ITS CREATORS 109

PART 2   THE APPLICATION 121

CHAPTER 9   THE PHOENIX DOG PISS THEORY 123

CHAPTER 10   BIG COMPANIES ARE LIKE BIG SHIPS—
SLOW TO MOVE AND SLOW TO CHANGE
131

CHAPTER 11   SYSTEMIZE THE ROUTINE; HUMANIZE
THE EXCEPTION 141

  YOU CAN TURN ANGRY CUSTOMERS INTO RAVING
  FANS SIMPLY BY SOLVING THEIR PROBLEMS
  142

CHAPTER 12   THE SINGLE EGG ORGANIZATION 151

  THE SINGLE EGG ORGANIZATION 154

  FEDERAL EXPRESS CREATES FEDEX SERVICES
  156

  LARSON-JUHL COMBINES SALES AND SERVICE
  LOCALLY 158

  BELL SPORTS SETS UP SEPARATE COMPANIES
  159

CHAPTER 13   THE HIERARCHY OF HORRORS 161

CHAPTER 14   THE SEVEN DYNAMICS OF CHANGE 171

  DYNAMICS OF CHANGE EXERCISE 172

  HOW TO DEAL WITH THE DYNAMICS OF CHANGE
  176

  THE TWO INGREDIENTS TO INNOVATIVE SUCCESS
  181

WHAT IS THE PROCESS AND HOW IS IT
    COMPATIBLE WITH SYSTEMS THINKING? 182
REDUCING THE WORKFORCE 184
THE HUDSON RIVER RUNWAY 185

PART 3   THE RESULTS 189

CHAPTER 15 THE PADDI LUND STORY 191
    THE COURTESY SYSTEM 206

CHAPTER 16 ANATOMY OF A START-UP: INNOVATION
    IN ACTION 209

CHAPTER 17 ANATOMY OF A TURNAROUND: CUSTOMER
    CULTURE IN TRANSITION 223

APPENDIX A THE VISION OF THE IDEAL AT A FEDERAL
    EXPRESS STATION 241
    THE FEDERAL EXPRESS STATION: AN IDEAL 243
    THE IDEAL STATION 243
    POSTSCRIPT 249

APPENDIX B THE UPS PHILOSOPHY AS STATED BY
    ITS FOUNDER 251
    QUOTES 254
    DETERMINED MEN 258

INDEX 267

FOREWORD

Mike Basch's part in the history of corporate America is extraordinary.

He has been involved in big, exciting corporate businesses like UPS and Federal Express that deal annually with customers in the millions. Looking back, Mike's role and principle responsibility in these legendary businesses has been to create a strong CustomerCulture, although it was not called that at the time, which has been integral to the long-term success and dominance of these companies in their respective industries.

Systems engineering, sales, customer service, corporate mission statements...they are all part of the mix of any modern day business, but only Mike sees clearly the relationship between these issues, a true CustomerCulture and the incredible company success of which corporate legends are made.

FROM ONE EXTREME TO ANOTHER

In contrast, I have a humble enterprise in a working-class suburb in Australia. It's flattering that Mike would ask me to write this forward and would feature my business as a prominent example of his principles in action. Perhaps I should briefly explain why.

Much has been said about me and my little dental business over the years, Mike being the keenest proponent. My business is successful and makes me more money than I can easily spend. I work three short days a week, and I love every minute I'm at the office—which is unusual given my profession.

My business is very small by most standards. Long ago I locked my front door and fired most of my customers, which is probably why I'm considered a little "crazy." I now have around 750 clients, in contrast to Mike's millions. Over time we have learned to treat our customers very well. Indeed, that is the sole reason we generate income so efficiently.

THE PROCESS OF CUSTOMER SUCCESS

I first met Mike when he visited my business a few years ago. He impressed me with his honesty and friendliness, as well as his depth of knowledge about business in general and customer service in particular.

Most people are intrigued with the sensational side of my story, but Mike better than anyone else has looked past that to study my business deeply. He identified clearly the process that led us to create the experience my customers now enjoy that brings them back time and again, and attracts their friends, family, and colleagues.

It is telling about Mike's insight and skills that he has managed to distill the essence of not just the customer-service ideas of my small business, but those of medium- and large-sized business as well. And I think you'll find his process for building that into a pervasive CustomerCulture to be quite exciting.

CUSTOMER SERVICE BY CHANCE

Unfortunately, I can't quite claim that I deliberately set out to create exactly what we achieved. My motivations were far simpler—I simply wanted customers to give me money more easily. Customer Service. That must be the answer, otherwise why would people want to come see a dentist. Perhaps you've experienced the same rationale?

Like most people, I must admit to doing only what seemed obvious at the time. I didn't have a process to follow, or a plan to reveal the path before me. But somewhere along the way, and after many years and many blind alleys, our customer service focus became a strong CustomerCulture. It's now instilled in all of our people and all that we do. I only wish I'd met Mike sooner!

CUSTOMER CULTURE BY DESIGN

In hindsight, I can see now that the central principles of great customer service are simple: Work out what it takes to make customers happy, implement systems to provide this happiness, show the team how it is to their advantage to follow the system, and continually measure and track your team's performance as you evolve to higher and higher levels of customer loyalty.

As you'll see in a little while, Mike identifies the steps in this process as **Vision, Values, Goals, Relevance, Action,** and **Feedback.** It seems so simple now! Unfortunately, the devil is in the detail, but Mike will hold your hand along the way, drawing on his vast experience with a broad range of ideas and theories.

My favorite is "The Phoenix Dog-Piss Theory" in Chapter 9. I must confess to being thoroughly delighted with this management gem. So much so that I decided to propound my own "Two Kangaroos Loose on the Barbie Hypothesis," which I think would be a great addition to Mike's next book.

Theories aside, deep down we all know how customers want to be treated...because we are all customers ourselves. We have all experienced the same problems that our own customers face, and we have taken our custom away from places where we did not feel welcomed.

You innately understand how creating a culture of treating customers exceptionally well can be a very effective way to grow businesses, create new markets, and dominate industries. Within the pages of this book lie the answers to many of the problems you'll face in doing just that.

Mike is a warm, caring human being, but also a savvy management mastermind with an eye for sifting the valuable diamonds from the otherwise functional bits of coal. Join him as he recounts his journey through corporate American history.

What you're about to learn could very well change your approach to work, and certainly has the capacity to transform your organization.

Dr. Paddi Lund, BDS, FRACDS
Patrick Lund's Dental Happiness

Introduction

Culture drives performance in an organization. Culture is everything. As one Chief Executive Officer (CEO) recently put it: "Get the culture right, and your people will do what is necessary to serve their customers and make owners piles of money." Put an average human being in an above-average culture, and the person will change behaviors to adapt to the new culture. Change the culture in an existing company, and the people will change with it.

An organizational culture is a system. That system can drive people to high performance directed toward profitable customer loyalty, or it can drive apathy, internally directed, or any number of destructive "customer cancerous" activities.

We are creatures of habit. Action and reaction are programmed early in life, and we respond the way that we have always responded, unless there is a change in the action/reaction structures, which are those structures that give us the opportunity to experience pleasure or to avoid pain.

Nearly all that we do is conditioned by habit, and habit is the result of culture. Build a culture where the behaviors you desire are clear and recognized, and people will gradually build habits around those behaviors. Then, the organization will habitually serve its customers with ever-increasing value.

People change, not because managers direct them to change, but because they find themselves in a culture where personal change is in their best interest.

Assuming you, as a corporate or group leader or even as an employee, want to become part of changing the way that people behave in some way, you must change the culture that these people operate in. In effect, you must change the system or the action/reaction paradigm that makes up your corporate (or family) culture.

People instinctively adapt to the culture they step into. If the culture is high performing, people will be high performing or will leave if they are not willing to perform to the cultural standards.

CustomerCulture is about consciously building the customer-centered organization where employees are focused on serving their customers (internal or external) for sustained, profitable growth.

Back to systems that drive our behaviors. Some simple examples of systems in action...

You step into a shower and turn the water on. With one hand in the water and the other on the valve, you gradually move the valve until the water is the right temperature. You sense the water temperature, unconsciously compare it to the temperature you desire, adjust the valve to change it if it's not right, and continue to go through this cycle until the temperature is right.

Over time, innovative people and manufacturers develop valves where, as a customer, you set the right temperature on the front end and simply turn the water on.

This is a simple example of how systems work and how customer focus evolves products and solutions to customers' needs.

Another example...

You're late for an important appointment. You get in your car and quickly accelerate up to the speed limit. You constantly look at the speedometer and press and release the gas pedal to reach the optimum speed. You observe the traffic and what is going on around you and take the necessary actions to minimize your time on the road and to meet your goal of getting to your appointment on time.

Over time, innovative people and manufacturers developed cruise control, and now you simply get your car up to speed and press the button to maintain the ideal speed. Your mind and behaviors can then concentrate on other issues, increasing your performance.

These are two simple examples of systems in action.

You have a **goal,** whether it is the right temperature or the right speed. The goal is **relevant** to you at the moment. You take **action** to meet the goal, and you get **feedback**. If the goal is not being met, the cycle continues with another action and feedback until you have reached equilibrium (satisfaction) in the process.

On a macro scale, this becomes an evolutionary process. You go through the **goal, relevance, action, feedback** cycle again and again in nearly everything you do. As you go through this cycle, you get inventive looking for solutions to make it simpler, easier, faster, less expensive, more comfortable, and so forth.

The people and companies that do this constantly are the evolutionary forces that continue to grow and innovate in their never-ending quest for finding better ways. This is the definition of CustomerCulture.

The purpose of this book is to (a) consciously develop cultural structures or systems to get your employees into this process and (b) look for better, more cost effective, and more valuable ways to serve your customers.

When you have every employee and every customer looking for ways to improve your effectiveness as an organization, you grow and thrive.

When these simple and natural cultural structures are given conscious direction in an organization, the organization performs at much higher levels. People have a sense of purpose and learn to work together to innovate and grow constantly.

A company or organization either grows or decays. There is no steady state over time. Change and growth is a core human need and phenomenon. It cannot be denied. It is possible, however, to set up the success structures to relearn your business every day.

This book is about getting conscious about understanding cultural structures and building and applying them in ways that enable you and your people to relearn your business every day, to help you constantly grow in delivering products and services focused on customers, products, and services that customers are willing to pay for and that make you lots of money.

CustomerCulture seeks to apply a systems foundation to your cultural structures and then to provide examples of how systems thinking built Federal Express, United Parcel Service (UPS), Larson-Juhl, a very exciting dental practice, a company turnaround, a start-up, and many other companies.

The principles discussed in this book go back nearly 100 years to UPS and its vision. They were then applied at Federal Express during its embryonic phase and currently are being applied by companies exercising these principles both in revamping existing cultures and starting up new businesses.

Federal Express is the primary example because I participated in the initial development of the culture from the ground up. The company's culture has withstood the test of time and continues to flourish against enormous competition from one of the best companies in their industry—UPS.

Little is known about UPS, but it is one of the strongest, if not the strongest, company in existence today. It is nearly 100 years old and has developed a business that makes nearly every career management employee (supervisors and higher) a millionaire by the time they retire. It has consistently performed through tough times, is relatively debt free, and has a very low employee turnover rate in an industry with high turnover. Finally, I defy anyone to catch a UPS driver napping on the job.

Larson-Juhl is a privately held midsized company (1,300 employees) that dominates its market for the manufacture and distribution of picture-framing products. Larson-Juhl is run by a visionary CEO who has demonstrated the success that comes from walking the talk when it comes to the values that drive an organization.

To round out the example companies with a smaller business, we use an eight-person dental office in Brisbane, Australia. Paddi Lund, the dentist, went from near suicide and working 60 hours a week making average dental pay to a by-invitation-only business.

This business makes two and a half times as much as the average dental office, locks its doors, took its name out of the phone book, and fired 75% of its customers. Paddi's book, *Building the Happiness Centered Business,* has been a favorite for the small business that wants a CustomerCulture. Many of his principles have been applied to larger businesses as well.

A couple of examples are also shown from organizations that have what we call a cancerous culture, a culture that drives people away from the customer and toward self-serving, destructive practices.

The principles in this book can be applied to family, nonprofit groups, or any number of other group activities where there is a desire to change behaviors to better meet the needs of the people who are part of the organization and its mission.

THE THEORY

This book is broken up into three parts: The Theory, The Application, and The Results.

This first part covers how the theory got formulated using the Federal Express start-up story as the primary example.

CustomerCulture is primarily about building an action/reaction culture where actions taken by employees are focused on customers. This part provides the theory and plenty of examples showing how the theory was developed and why it is a very practical way to run your organization or even to participate in an organization.

1

AMERICA, YOU HAVE A NEW AIRLINE AND...A NEW STANDARD OF SERVICE

I t was March 12, 1973. We had been working for years for this day—the first day of operations for Federal Express. We had 28 people selling in 10 cities since January 2, 1973. We had 23 executive jet airplanes (10 of which had been converted to freighters); hundreds of employees; a hub and World War II facilities in Memphis, TN; and no money.

Frederick W. Smith, the founder, had used all of his family's trust fund and incredible banking and leasing salesmanship to get us here, but that was all there was.

Fred Smith, myself, and others had traveled to New York and had appointments with venture capitalists all around the city the next day. Fred had seen most of these venture capitalists earlier, and they had told him to come back when we were in business. Now we were, and we were ready.

I was Senior Vice President of Sales and Customer Service. That meant setting up the pickup and delivery operation, along with the sales and service operations.

Each evening, for the past two and a half months, we had a conference call to review the results of the sales calls for the day, and we'd track the expected number of packages the first night. By mid-February, we were estimating as high as 3,000 packages for that first night.

The problem, at that level, was that our planes only held 300 packages each, and most of the 10 airplanes were contracted to the post office and other charter commitments. We could cancel contracts and deploy all 10 airplanes, but it would be very costly and risky if we didn't actually get 3,000 packages.

I decided that we'd better verify that the customer commitments were real. I started asking more specific questions and found out that sometimes salespeople lie, or at least tell you what you want to hear.

For example, one of the shippers from Memphis was a brick company that was supposed to give us 20 packages a day. I asked the salesperson why they were using an overnight service. "Are they going to ship samples to architects?" He replied, "No, they're shipping bricks to the construction site."

I knew we were in trouble. After nearly a week of probing, we had changed our estimate to 300 packages. This was perfect: two airplanes averaging 150 packages each at 50% capacity. We were off and running.

America, you have a new airline.

On that opening Monday night, the Memphis hub was alive with local and national TV, the *Wall Street Journal,* and local newspapers. It was the first new airline in America in 20 years, and certainly the first all-package airline ever. It was newsworthy stuff.

It was 10:00 p.m. on that Monday in March, and we had just arrived at the Yale Club in New York City. I called Memphis to get the actual package count and asked John Henry, "What's the package count?"

"Are you sitting down?"

"Should I be?"

"Well, there's good news and bad news," he replied.

"Give me the good news."

"Single digit—six packages."

"John," I replied, totally shocked, "what could possibly be the bad news?"

"Four were from salespeople testing the system. Only two from customers."

Can you picture it? Dozens of people out in the middle of the night, the media, conveyors, spotlights washing WWII ramps and hangars with light. The first plane pulls up, the cargo door swings open, and two pilots, each with a package in his hands, passes it to the awaiting throng—a throng expecting two full airplanes or at least half-full airplanes.

Back in New York, after getting the news, I walked down the hall to Fred Smith's room and knocked timidly. I told him the news, and we had a brief discussion about what we were going to do with the rest of our lives because this wasn't going to work.

The next morning Fred had recovered. As we settled into a taxi to begin our venture capital tour, he looked at each of us and said, "Fix bayonets. We're in the trenches now. Our dream is a reality. Let's make it happen."

There was such an incredible sense of commitment from Fred that we did a reasonable job of explaining why we had spent two and a half months with 28 salespeople to get two packages.

I say reasonable because we didn't get thrown out, nor did we generate any capital.

As we were riding to our first appointment, one of the attorneys said, "Take heart. The first night is always rough. You'll have dozens of packages by Friday." On Friday of that week, we had one package in the system. I calculated the cost of that package at about $500,000 to deliver—a heck of a value to the shipper.

The immediate and very profound vision for all Federal Express people was spawned that first day:

GET THE PACKAGES.

This was my second experience with the power of vision. It was so crystal clear, but it was far more immediate than the "Determined people create their conditions. They are not the victims of them," which was and still is the UPS vision.

The power was the incredible motivation to do whatever was necessary on the part of hundreds of employees each with their own interpretation of what it would take to GET THE PACKAGES.

Packages meant growth, customers who bought our story, venture capitalists listening, financing, and so forth. Everything would happen with packages. Nothing would happen without them. Thousands of people would eventually have that same vision while we struggled, without money, for years to survive and finally to succeed and thrive.

Pilots would land their planes and go make sales calls. Other pilots would run pickup and delivery stations all focused on GET THE PACKAGES. Couriers (drivers) would build relationships with shipping clerks and go through our competitors' packages, pull off their airbills, and put ours on. We called them package thieves (a good term, although we didn't direct them to do it).

Looking back, I don't believe Federal Express would have become the industry leader that it is had we gotten the 300 packages. Without the sense of failure and the core learning that comes from failure, we would not have had the focus, nor would we have developed the service culture that still permeates the company today, nearly 30 years later.

We decided that first week that the 10 cities from Jacksonville, FL, to St. Louis, MO, didn't give shippers enough coverage. We identified 15 additional cities, including New York, Boston, Chicago, and other major cities in the east.

We put a team together with the mission to get 15 cities opened in 15 business days. The team would fly into a city with specific roles. One person took care of the Piper Cub and found a motel for everyone, another found a place for the cargo jet to unload and be serviced, another found a place for the trucks and couriers, and the fourth would go...to a bar during happy hour.

This last person was responsible for hiring. At the peak of happy hour activity, he'd stand on a chair, tap on a glass, and make the announcement that he was representing a new company in town and was hiring tonight. People would come to the table, fill out an application, and be hired on the spot. As Tom Peters says, "Hire fast; fire fast." And that's what we did.

The GET THE PACKAGES vision permeated at every level of the organization. People interpreted this vision each in their own way, and this gave us the strength that eventually made us unbeatable in the marketplace.

One such example...

One of the new cities we opened during that first month was a small town in Indiana. The only reason we decided to serve it was that it had an RCA plant that shipped 20 packages a day. By the time we got the additional 15 cities opened, April 17, 1973, we had 40 packages a day, so that would mean 50% growth—exciting.

So, we sent one of our best salespeople there with instructions to GET THE PACKAGES from RCA and to call when he had received the commitment and the packages.

He called me that first day and said the traffic manager wouldn't see him. I suggested that he get a good book and wait in the lobby all month until the guy would see him.

He called the next afternoon and said that he finally saw the traffic manager at 3:30 p.m. after waiting in the lobby all day and that the man wasn't going to switch carriers.

I asked why.

"He claims that everyone says they have overnight service. He's satisfied that no one delivers on the promise, and there's nothing I could say to him to convince him otherwise. I think he's being paid off by our competitor."

Sometimes, salespeople say that as a last resort.

"Did you offer him free service for the week? Did you offer to ship empty boxes so he could test the system and our promise? Did you explain the hub system and that we have our own airplanes?" I was desperately trying to figure out why people didn't believe us. This guy wasn't the first and, as I was learning, wouldn't be the last.

"I did all of that and more. I'm telling you, Mike, he's not going to use us."

"Okay, see if you can get a plane tomorrow to Boston. We need more salespeople there."

I'd like to say Federal Express had built a strong service ethic by design, but the reality is that we learned a number of very valuable lessons in the early days, most of which were taught to us by our employees.

Fred Smith had started with a People–Profit ethic. The idea was to focus on employees, and they would produce the profit. He wanted to build a different kind of company. Back in the 70s, people were numbers to large companies. Companies didn't care about their people. Fred wanted to build a people-first company. I had added the word "Service" to the mix, so the mantra had become and still is today: People—Service—Profit.

That was all well and good, but we needed PACKAGES and we needed them NOW.

One of the most valuable lessons was the power of people when they have a common vision and commitment. In this case, the vision was GET THE PACKAGES, and everyone understood it. In many cases, they understood it a lot more than I or other senior managers did, as this example demonstrates.

All kinds of things began to happen, but the biggest lesson in those early days was taught to me by a tracing clerk named Diane. Diane wasn't very busy tracing things because we had so many people and so few packages. It was pretty hard to screw things up in those early days.

Imagine Atlanta, GA, with five drivers and three packages. The couriers would jump over one another for something to deliver and, more often than not, the package would arrive at its destination before the person receiving it. Great service. The people getting the packages loved it and told our people so, and that made our people strive even harder for the recognition.

On a Friday afternoon, about two weeks after we opened the new cities, Diane got a call from a woman from the small town in Indiana, the town with the RCA plant that wouldn't use us.

The woman was crying and through the tears managed to get out:

"I don't know who Federal Express is. All I know is that my wedding dress was in Jacksonville, FL, yesterday, and you were supposed to deliver it by noon today. It's 3:30 p.m., and it's not here! I'm getting married tomorrow, and because we're a small town, it's the social event of the season. More important, it's the event of my life. Can you help me?"

Diane related to the problem and told the woman she'd call her back. Then, she used our tracing system at the time—call each station (there were only 25) and see if one has a package that doesn't belong in its station. On the sixth call, she found the package in Detroit, more than 300 miles away.

Now, she had a problem to solve. She was going to get the package delivered that afternoon. There wasn't a doubt in Diane's mind. All of us were out trying to sell shippers or investors, so there was no one in management to ask. Looking back, I'm not sure that she would have asked permission anyway. She was committed to getting the package delivered.

She lined up a Cessna and a pilot to fly the package to Wilmington, IN, of course. Any frontline employee would do that. After all, this woman was getting married.

On Monday morning, Diane received a call from the woman who was on her honeymoon in Mexico (not an easy task in those days to get a call placed from Mexico). The woman told Diane she had gotten her dress, described the wedding, and thanked her. Then, she asked if she could talk with a senior manager to relate the story. Diane transferred the call to me.

The woman described what had happened and what Diane had done for her. There were tears in her voice.

As she was describing Diane's actions, tears and all, all I could see was dollar signs. "How much did this cost?" I asked myself silently. As the woman went on, I scribbled a note to talk with Diane right after the call. After all, I had grown up with UPS. When a customer had a problem, you did what you could, but renting a plane wasn't on the list.

Then the woman gave me a clue that I didn't pick up until later, "Mr. Basch, it wasn't all good news. There was bad news also."

She got my attention. "Was it wrinkled?" I asked.

"Yes, but that's typical. We ironed it. The bad news was that I wasn't the center of attention at my own wedding. I had told a few people about my wedding dress having its own airplane, and the word spread. Pretty soon, the topic of discussion was this outrageous new airline for packages that had a plane per package." She laughed as she related the story.

I still wasn't laughing. I was still thinking about the cost and Diane gone astray, and then I envisioned hundreds of employees hiring planes and pilots at random. However, like all vice presidents, I was polite, thanked her for the call, and then went down the hall to find Diane.

"Why on earth would you charter a plane for a wedding dress?" I asked seriously.

"You said 'GET THE PACKAGES' and, for me, that means you give great service and solve the customer's problem. Then they talk about you, and you get more business."

Today, that makes enormous sense to me, but then it went totally over my head. "Come on Diane, if we spent $300 for every package, we'd go bankrupt."

After a couple of minutes of her attempting vainly to explain what GET THE PACKAGES meant to her and, in her fervent belief, what it meant to the company, she finally blurted out in total frustration:

"I figured we're going bankrupt anyway. What's the difference?"

There was obvious truth in that statement, so I let it go. Being people first meant honesty, and Diane was no stranger to our financial situation.

Two weeks later, RCA started giving us 20 packages a day.

A couple of their executives were at the wedding, and they went back and asked their traffic manager if he knew about Federal Express. One executive, in particular, made it plain that he should at least try our service. He did, and they began using Federal Express on a regular basis.

If I'd had a tail, it would have been between my legs as I went down to Diane's desk to relate the news. She had a smile on her face as I arrived telling me clearly, but at least silently, that she already knew about the RCA packages.

It was an incredible lesson—one of thousands of lessons learned in those early days. The biggest lesson was that if you were clear about what you wanted as leaders and then let people give it to you without tying their hands behind their backs, you got it. Often, you got it in ways you didn't expect, such as chartering an airplane for one package, but you got it.

The bottom line: We learned through failure, and failure is the **feedback** of a well-designed (either consciously or unconsciously) system. More important, our people had the freedom and the focus, GET THE PACKAGES, to use that feedback to take the necessary **actions** to achieve the **goal**.

I've been involved in 13 start-ups, and it's always the same. The feedback is so tied to the customer that people do whatever is required to meet the goals and succeed. That's why I find start-ups so stimulating. The systems cycle of **goal/relevance/action/feedback** is natural and is not clouded by politically driven motivations that get in the way of success.

Some companies, such as UPS, Federal Express, Cisco, Prentice Hall, and many others, have built the success structures to take them forward into megacompanies that don't lose sight of the customer. This book is about building those success structures.

We didn't get capital until that November, but we survived because we had commitment. During the summer of 1973, 600 employees received a pay envelope with their checks and a note. "Please don't cash the check because there's no money in the bank, but hang in there. We'll succeed together."

Only a handful of people left.

Many other things came with that commitment. Railway Express Agency (REA), a major competitor, went out of business, and we were able to capture the lion's share of its customers. United Airlines went on strike, leaving our air freight forwarder competitors without the ability to move freight, and our volume increased.

Fred Smith went to Las Vegas and won $29,000 on the blackjack tables—enough to meet payroll for another week.

A pilot used his personal credit card to pay a fuel bill and get the sheriff's patrol car out from in front of the airplane. A driver hocked his watch to purchase fuel to complete his deliveries. There were hundreds of stories of employees going far beyond the call of duty to deliver absolutely positively overnight when they didn't get much support from the top.

This was because the natural system of goal/relevance/action/ feedback was functioning flawlessly.

Probably the most outrageous story was a last-ditch effort in July 1973. We were out of money, our creditors were out of patience, and there was no light at the end of the tunnel. Most of us in senior management gave up once a week in those days. Then we'd run into Fred and walk away believing we were about to conquer the world.

I only saw Fred give up twice in three years, and in July 1973 he had given up. His first principle of finance was no longer working: "When you borrow, borrow big. Then, when things go wrong, you have partners instead of creditors."

Well, things had gone wrong. Our lawyers and accountants had done all they could do to hold off the creditors, but it was all over. It was Saturday morning, and, if we didn't have $1 million in the bank by open of business Monday morning, we were out of business. Fred had given up. He was ready to close the doors on Monday morning.

As a last-ditch effort, one of our attorneys had arranged a one-hour meeting in Chicago that afternoon with Henry Crown, the majority shareholder of General Dynamics. Henry had never heard of Fred or Federal Express. Fred had one hour to deliver a presentation and walk away with a $1 million cashier's check, or we were done. Talk about sales pressure.

Fred sold an option to purchase 80% of the company for a down payment of $1 million, and we stayed alive through the summer and into the fall until the venture capital came in—the first of three financing rounds that, at that time, represented the biggest venture capital start-up in American history.

Today, or at least during the .com bonanza, the $120 million we raised is a drop in the bucket, but, during those days, it was an enormous undertaking. Not making a profit for three years was not in the dictionary of the venture people.

When looking back, it was traumatic and, I believe, necessary.

Interestingly what would have been worse is to have gotten the 300 packages that first night. I believe we would have gotten sloppy about service and customer focus. Because we had just two customer packages, we became obsessed as a company with GETTING THE PACKAGES.

This vision didn't come in the form of a mandate from on high. It was blatantly obvious that PACKAGES were our only hope, although actions were taken by management to make it crystal clear to everyone. That obsession led to a strong service culture that has lasted decades and gets stronger all the time.

Federal Express' obsession with the conscious development of customer-focused systems and the use of technology has enabled it to maintain market share in the face of ruthless competition.

Fortunately, money or no, we had to build systems to maintain airplanes and flight rules, and that led to building systems for nearly every part of the operation.

Maintaining the spirit of the entrepreneurial company while doubling every year and moving toward bigness is a formidable task and can only be accomplished by systematizing nearly every part of the operation, from how people get to their jobs to how packages are sorted and tracked to what planes fly where and who flies them.

By systems here, we don't mean just information systems, but rather cause-and-effect systems. If this choice is made, this is the likely outcome. People are driven primarily by systems as used in this context. Well-designed systems tie choice and actions to outcome.

For example, if an organization recognizes certain behaviors, more of those behaviors will occur over time. If the recognition is for behaviors not desired, nonetheless, more of those negative behaviors will occur. If Diane were ridiculed for getting the wedding dress to the wedding, the service ethic at Federal Express would have turned into a cost focus leading to relatively poor service over time and continued dominance by UPS, even in the air business.

I will show some of the changes Federal Express has made through the years to remain customer focused as it continues to grow from two packages that first night to more than 4 million packages (just Federal Express express air packages) today.

The overall lesson for our current economy is that only your employees can keep you innovating and evolving constantly, or only your employees can contract the deadly disease of Customer Cancer. Only well-designed goal/relevance/action/feedback systems can optimize your employees' focus on giving power to customers.

Customer Cancer is a term I use to express organizational systems run amuck. Instead of customer focus, the cells or employees begin to focus on each other or on themselves rather than the greater good where everyone wins.

Customer Cancer is not a disease caused by competitors, by government regulation, or the economy. It is a disease of indifference, poor focus by corporate leaders, and the lack of CustomerCulture. Customer Cancer is a disease that is contracted only from within.

Human cancer research has shown that, "Unlike normal body cells, they [cancer cells] disregard the needs of the community of cells. They are selfish and unsociable and are only interested in their own proliferative advantage."

An example of Customer Cancer in a related organization is the United States Postal Service (USPS).

A contractor friend of mine was walking with the postmaster through a local post office preparing to bid on some construction work. He spotted a $20 bill on the floor and began to stoop down to pick it up when the postmaster held him back and explained, "That is bait to catch thieves. The mirror you see over there is a two-way mirror, and there's a security guard watching to see who picks it up."

It's no wonder postal service employees are not customer focused. It is not easy to change a culture that ingrained and that large, but, starting with one postal facility at a time, it is possible, and it must start with a degree of employee trust. Certainly both UPS and Federal Express have their share of employee theft, but there are far better ways of handling it than tempting honest employees to find $20. That is Customer Cancer.

This same phenomenon happens in companies that don't walk the talk when it comes to focusing on employee and customer well-being. I have yet to talk with or even hear about CEOs that don't say employees and customers were their primary focus. The problem is that 95% talk about it and 5% demonstrate it through their employees' actions and behaviors. It is those behaviors that reflect the prevailing culture, not the platitudes of senior managers.

Fred Smith had several thoughts on this subject:

"Give employees a sense of control over their own destiny, and they'll do anything you ask—and more." Systems must be designed to give employees and customers control of their relationship with you and their customers.

"When an employee wants a raise, only the customer can grant it. It is up to the employees to figure out how to add enough additional value to get the customer to pay for it. Customers will pay if there is value. Stockholders won't." Systems provide the reward and the focus for employees to understand this reality and to constantly look for ways to add value to the customer's experience.

"The sun will not set on an unresolved customer or employee problem, meaning that, if the problem cannot be resolved, at least it will be dealt with and the people involved will be aware that it is being dealt with." Systems provide the sense of urgency.

On his second comment, being people first doesn't mean being the parent and entitling employees to all the benefits and rewards without accountability and performance. It doesn't mean taking care of people, but rather demanding the best from every person.

This book shows how many companies have been able to build power with customer focus. It also shows how focus on products and engineering at the expense of the customer (Customer Cancer) will gradually mean the decline of big business in favor of a more distributed model.

Being customer focused is a must in the new economy. Those company leaders that believe it is not will lose. The Internet just may be the asteroid that kills the dinosaur.

CustomerCulture uses the Federal Express story and other reference stories to drive home the importance of systems.

These reference stories act as springboards to creating a positive customer experience by demonstrating the power and need for the underlying systems that focus employees on customers—an experience that parallels the experience of the woman from the small town in Indiana.

It's no longer about customer service. It's about congruent and continuous customer experiences driven by culturalizing nearly every interaction. This means systematizing the routine and humanizing the exception. It means having all employees vitally aware of the need for customer loyalty, whether they design computer screens, fly airplanes, manufacture things, or pay expense accounts.

If the experience is bad, we'll see Customer Cancers developing. If it is good, we have customer health and longevity.

The Federal Express story told in this chapter is nearly 30 years old, but the principles and the stories told in subsequent chapters underline the cultural principles that have made and are making companies throughout the world great today.

2

SYSTEMS DRIVE PEOPLE

rdinary people working with extraordinary systems deliver extraordinary results. To put it another way, systems, not people, drive 95% of what goes on within an organization. I realize that this is a lot to swallow right up front, but read on to see why I make such a bold statement.

If you want to change your results, you change your cultural systems.

Obviously, we are not talking about just information or computer systems. We are talking about a much broader view of systems—cultural systems. The culture we live in is a system. A system is cause and effect: If this, then that. The cultural structure is the system that drives a given organization and the behavior of its people.

People learn very quickly what is acceptable within an organization and what is not. More important, they learn and act on those things that give them their greatest personal reward. If that action is in alignment with corporate goals, the organization and the people benefit. If it is not in alignment, the organization and its people suffer.

Most of peoples' learning and behavior is unconscious to them and driven by the system that is in place called the culture. They are reacting within the system to a set of norms and consequences established by the system. Choice is generally tied to outcome in some way, but for the most part, it is unconscious.

For example, if people are applauded for going out of their way to serve a customer the way that Diane did at Federal Express (see Chapter 1) by getting the wedding dress delivered against all obstacles, more and more people will go out of their way to serve customers in extraordinary ways. This was very clear in the beginning days of Federal Express where people took outrageous actions that eventually led to a customer-centric culture.

On the other hand, if people go out of their way to serve a customer and no benefits accrue for them and no recognition is given, fewer and fewer people will go out of their way to serve. Eventually, the norm of poor service is established (Customer Cancer), and, try as they might, management cannot change that norm through conventional techniques.

This is especially true in today's environment where people are extremely busy and must choose how they spend their time and what they focus on.

This norm can only be changed by changing the underlying cultural structures. Companies focusing on these structures are able to establish a great advantage in the marketplace.

McDonald's, for example, catapulted to number 1 in fast food because of systems—systems or cultures that are pervasive in every outlet. It holds that advantage today even though many of its competitors have duplicated its systems. Often, the company that leads with good systems establishes an unconquerable edge.

Wal-Mart is supply-chain systems driven. Its job is to keep the shelves full at the lowest possible cost, and Wal-Mart does it well. If a product begins moving faster than predicted, flags go up, the movement is investigated, and measures are taken to speed up the supply chain for that specific product. Its systems are customer responsive and very efficient.

Federal Express withstood the onslaught of incredible competition from UPS and others that delivered with the same reliability because of better customer-centered information systems, particularly the ability to give people the peace of mind that comes from knowing where their package is.

On the other hand, UPS continues to dominate the total package delivery scene (ground and air combined) because of superior delivery management systems and the cost advantage that gives them.

Now, let's take a look at how systems work effectively to accomplish corporate goals. The cultural structure design shown here shows cause and effect. It works for a raccoon in search of food, a person attempting to lose weight, a government attempting to resolve a societal problem, or an organization attempting to improve customer focus.

Well-designed cultural structures have six primary attributes:

1. **Vision**: A clear picture of the desired customer experience

2. **Values**: The code of conduct or rules of the game that will not be compromised

3. **Goals**: The specific time-critical results that the organization desires to achieve

4. **Relevance**: The desire or determination level among the people to achieve goals

5. **Feedback**: The results or scoreboard that tells people their relative success

6. **Actions**: The specific actions taken by the people to achieve the goals

We show actions last here to emphasize that, if all else is in place, people's actions will be directed by vision and focused on achieving the goals within the established values.

Given actions focused on achieving the goals with determination, the corporation cannot help but succeed.

The interaction between these attributes is shown in Figure 2–1.

The vision provides the light and the gravitational force. The vision is the compass of the enterprise—its purpose for being. More practically and specifically, it is the experience that the organization is attempting to create for its customers, employees, and owners. What will success look like as an experience for the constituents that must be served?

That experience is then condensed into a headline that provides direction, as in the following examples:

"A chicken in every pot."

—F. D. Roosevelt during the Depression

"A man on the moon by the end of the decade."

—J. F. Kennedy in the 1960s

"Absolutely, Positively, Overnight."

—Federal Express

"Determined people make conditions. They are not the victims of them."

—Jim Casey, UPS

Values provide the boundaries. It is often possible to accomplish the vision by compromising the means, journey, or balance. Values are designed to provide the rules of the game. They are the boundaries that, when violated, call for a reassessment of the actions.

Goals are the deliverables within a given timeframe that need to be all encompassing to focus on customers, employees, and owners.

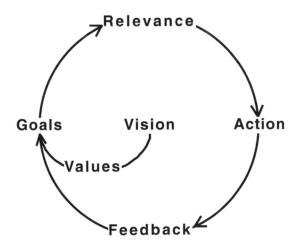

FIGURE 2–1
Culture system diagram.

Relevance makes achieving the goals important to the people who are responsible for their achievement. If the goals are not personally relevant to the action players, they will not be achieved, or, if achieved, they will not be achieved in a consistently productive way. Relevance includes incentives, recognition, attention, or focus by managers, and other ways of providing positive and motivating consequences to people when goals are achieved.

Actions are the doing activities to achieve the goals. If all else is in place, actions happen automatically to achieve the goals, and the corporation continually evolves to higher and higher levels of success. If the actions are counterproductive, a systemic cause is in one or more of the other five structural attributes.

Feedback lets the action players know the results of their actions. They are either achieving their goals, or they are not. If they are, the actions that they are taking are worthwhile. If not, actions will change automatically if the goals are clear and relevant and the feedback shows people the results of their actions.

The circle of cause and effect continues on and on. If goals are being achieved, the actions will not change much until the goals change. If they are not, actions will change in order to continue to meet the goals.

Another way to put it is that after the organization's purpose and values are clear, the well-designed system simply provides a reaction for every action and the appropriate actions happen as a matter of course.

The CEO and top managers set the vision and values. They set the goal categories that will meet the needs of customers, employees, and owners. They set the policies that govern much of the relevance function. They ensure that the necessary processes are implemented to give people feedback.

The direct manager's function, in this context, is to participate in actual goal setting to make the established goals clear and to focus on the accepted goals, making them relevant. The direct manager then provides feedback to people as a coach would provide feedback to players. The players can see the scoreboard, but are more productive when they receive feedback as to the meaning of the score to them personally and as a team.

Nearly every corporate problem has, at its core, a systemic cause going to one or more of the six attributes of a good cultural structure.

Most sports provide examples of good systems. In football, for example, the vision might be to be the best team possible. The rules of the game (values) are clear to all the players and their managers and cannot be violated without penalty. Goals are very clear. Ten yards equals a first down, a touchdown equals six points, and so on. The team with the most points wins and so forth.

The scoreboard provides feedback on an immediate and continuing basis. The coach provides feedback on the process for each player and the team as a whole. The coach also helps make the goals relevant to the players by continuing to focus on the vision and the goals.

Achieving the goals is also made relevant by peoples' natural desire to excel and to win. This is as true in business as it is in sports, if not more so.

As a result of good systems' design, sports are rightly held up as a model for business. All too often, however, sports are used for the relevance or motivational aspects of the system while ignoring the values, goals, and feedback attributes of sport.

Therefore, the bottom line for building an effective cultural structure is to establish a vision, make the rules clear, set goals, build relevance into the goals, and provide good and continuous feedback. When all these attributes are in place, people will take the actions necessary to achieve the goals that are relevant to them.

In most of the companies we have worked with, lack of feedback and relevance seems to be the cause of most cultural failures, the Customer Cancer.

Most companies have a vision, albeit more often unstated, and most have values and goals. Few have strong feedback systems that let people know the score on a regular basis, and most relevance practices push people toward suboptimizing the power of people and the organization.

A UPS Systems Example: Reducing Transaction Costs...

Think about the last time you observed a UPS driver not working at a fast pace. Now consider the management challenge of managing 350,000 people—most of whom you see for just a brief time every morning and evening, people who spend 90% of their time essentially in their own business of pickup and delivery.

This example illustrates how UPS accomplishes this task day in and day out with a strong cultural structure.

Background

UPS has always focused on goals and feedback as the key ingredients to good management. Before computers, managers were armed with both daily and weekly operating reports that gave them feedback about their performance and the performance of the people under their supervision.

If managers didn't know their cost per package during the previous week or which drivers were not performing well, they were not seen as good managers, nor were they seen as "determined people."

The UPS vision was "Determined people make conditions. They are not the victims of them. Determined people, working together, can accomplish anything."

Even a small operating center with 12 drivers would employ a part-time clerk four hours each night to compile the numbers for each driver each day into a spreadsheet-like operating report showing each driver's performance.

Because of the overriding vision, there was only one reason for poor performance. You and your people, or at least some of your people, were not determined.

Good service was defined as flawless service (package on time) and low cost (at a price the customer was willing to pay).

PROBLEM

I was brought into a district where productivity had fallen substantially. The cultural structure, so successful in other areas, was not working in this district. The numbers were being compiled every day, and the information was there, but the managers were not using the information to provide feedback and to build relevance.

The district was driven by a very strong union, and managers had acquiesced to the power of the union.

We had to change the culture to focus people on reducing costs while maintaining on-time delivery. We set a cost-reduction goal of moving delivery costs from 28 cents to 23 cents per package relevant to the frontline people (drivers) who had to change their actions in order to meet the goal.

SYSTEMIC CAUSE

The cause of the problem was lack of relevance. The company's goals were not relevant to the people who had to achieve them—the pickup and delivery drivers.

The goals were clear to management, and the feedback systems were in place, but the managers were not using the scoreboard to convey the importance and relevance of meeting the goals to the drivers. They were driven by another relevance policy—the union.

SOLUTION

As industrial engineering manager, I set up a new system at the district headquarters where I employed two part-time clerks to gather information from 28 operating centers each night. The clerks from each center called in and reported on key indexes each night from each center. These numbers were then rolled up into division information.

Each morning at 10 a.m. I conducted a conference call with the four division managers responsible for the 28 centers.

I had no authority to direct, only to ask questions. These questions would, over time, make the goals relevant to everyone involved.

My focus was primarily on productivity, so I asked questions like: Who was most over standard in Yorktown yesterday (meaning which driver had the poorest performance)? When was the last time the center manager rode with him or her? What was your cost per package last week in Haverstown?

To make this system even more relevant to the division managers on the call, our district manager sat in once in a while unannounced and created all kinds of grief when the division managers didn't have the answers.

Interestingly, in the beginning, none of the division managers had the answers, but, after several weeks, it was difficult to ask a question without getting an immediate answer. The division managers began anticipating the questions and asking their center managers before our call. The center managers began to anticipate the questions and ask the drivers when they reported for work that morning.

It wasn't long before every person was focused on his or her own performance, whether manager or driver.

In addition to this simple, daily system, center managers and division managers were recognized for moving toward the goal each week. They, in turn, recognized the drivers that had improved their performance.

RESULT

The net result of this performance-improving system was a cost-per-package reduction from 28 cents per package to 23 cents per package in six months, which was a 20% reduction in costs.

This is cause-and-effect systems thinking. In this case, we used feedback to make goals relevant to people. They took the actions necessary to build performance and to achieve the goals.

POSTSCRIPT

Under this new system, if you as a division manager are aware of your performance and the performance of those working with you, you will be recognized positively. This is no different than a football team meeting its goal of a first down. Everyone wins when systems keep people focused on goals and informed about results.

This cost-reduction project was an example of a system designed to focus people on one aspect of their business. A system came together to focus people on cost-driven performance in this case. This particular approach put relevance into a system with clear goals and feedback. After these attributes of a good structure were all working well, people at every level took the actions necessary to improve performance.

All too often managers see their job as training people to take the proper actions. Good cultural structures motivate people to take the actions that they know will achieve the goals. If training is necessary, that becomes one of the actions taken.

Poor structures leave people apathetic or focusing on personal rather than organizational goals.

Nearly 10 years later, I applied this same technique of daily conference calls when running the southern division for Federal Express. The results were the same, taking the division from number three and four in all performance categories to one and two in less than one year.

ANOTHER UPS EXAMPLE: AN ELEGANT SOLUTION TO REDUCE MIS-SORTS

BACKGROUND

UPS, as well as Federal Express, the USPS, and every other national package carrier, uses hubs to move packages from source to use. Packages are picked up remotely, moved into a central sorting area, sorted to destination vehicles (whether planes or trucks), and then transported to centers for delivery.

In this example, UPS had a major hub in Philadelphia. Knowing which packages go where is critical to getting packages to their destination on time. In the case of Philadelphia, the sorting operators had to learn 10,000 cities and towns in Pennsylvania and New Jersey and get them to the right transport vehicle.

The Philadelphia hub had what was called a primary sort where 40 people would sort packages by looking at the city/town and state (before zip codes) and convert the location in their mind to a three-digit sort code. They would then place the package on a conveyor for the area represented by the three-digit code. The conveyor would transport the package to the proper truck for transport to the operating center.

For example, Harrisburg, PA, might have a 390 code, and the proper conveyor would have 390, along with other center codes, on it.

PROBLEM

More than 10% of the packages were placed on the wrong conveyor and had to be loaded in trucks on the perimeter of the sorting operation and brought back to the central sort for re-sorting. This delayed the outbound transport trucks at the end of the night, leading to poor service and increased costs.

After some investigation, it was determined that most of the sorters did not know the sort and could not make the mental conversion from city and state to the three-digit code.

SYSTEMIC CAUSE

The goals were clear: No mis-sorts and on-time departures. Feedback was fair. Managers knew how many packages were being rehandled each night, although they could not pinpoint exactly which sorters had the mis-sorts.

Again, the cause was lack of relevance. The people sorting the packages simply didn't care whether they knew the cities or sorted the packages properly, and there was not a good way to pinpoint exactly which sorters caused the problem (individual feedback).

SOLUTION

Not understanding cultural structures at that time, I took a more conventional approach: Teach the sorters the relationship between cities and the three-digit sort code.

I had spent a day preparing study sheets that I would hand out to the sorters, have them study for a while, and then test them on their ability to write the appropriate sort code next to the city— a typical teaching method.

I'll never forget the first night in the sort. The manager had set aside an hour with six of the sorters for me to teach. I walked in and explained the process to six people with crossed arms and surly attitudes.

Essentially they said, "We don't have to learn this sort. There's nothing in our union contract to make us." When I passed out the study sheets, no one even looked at them.

I had come from a district where employees cared. This was an older district and, again, run by the union more than management. Neither managers nor the frontline people were determined to meet the goals.

Frustrated, I called corporate the next day to get some suggestions. Others had to have experienced the same problem and had to have a way to solve it. They suggested flash cards. Show a city to the group and get them to call out the code. "Make it competitive and fun," they said.

That night I tried flash cards with the same response. It was embarrassing holding up card after card to a silent audience with smirks on their face.

An ex-union steward from the hub, Mario Umile, had been promoted to the industrial engineering department. The next morning I went to him. "You know these guys. What will it take to teach them the sort?"

Mario smiled. "You don't understand the problem. You believe the problem is how to teach them whereas the problem is really how to motivate them to learn the sort."

"OK," I replied, "so how do I motivate them to learn?"

"I don't know, but give me a day, and I'll come up with something."

The next day he came in with a stack of 3 × 5 cards. In fact, there were a couple of hundred of them. When I asked what he was planning to do with them, he suggested we go into the sort that night together, and he would show me in practice.

That night, Mario and I went into the class together, and I let him take the lead. He had a box with the 3 × 5 cards and poker chips.

"Guys, we're going to play poker tonight. On these cards are the names of cities and towns in Pennsylvania and New Jersey. You can win by having a pair of 490s as long as you know the sort codes. If you play a pair and you are challenged and get them wrong, you lose the hand even though you still may have had a winning hand."

He went on. "It's against company policy to gamble with money, so I brought poker chips along to make the game more fun, but you can't equate these to real money. I've put a value on each chip just for fun."

He passed out $100 worth of chips to each person, selected 52 cards from the pile of cards, and handed them to one of the sorters, who shuffled and dealt out 5 cards to each person. The first night was funny as the sorters spent most of the time arguing about cities and codes. We just sat there with the study sheets, let them argue for a while, and then settled the arguments with the proper city-code translation.

Every sorter wanted a study sheet to take home that night. The next night every sorter in the building wanted a study sheet.

RESULT

Within days, the sorters in class had learned the sort and, within a couple of weeks, every sorter in the building had learned the sort. Mis-sorts fell to less than 2% within a month.

POSTSCRIPT

After the first night, Mario pulled me aside and said, "Mike, you heard me tell them no gambling, but mark my word. They will work out a way to figure out who owes what to whom and settle during breaks."

Sure enough, there were indications of money changing hands, which all of us ignored. Making goals relevant can often take some interesting twists.

The general question is: What would make this goal relevant to the people who have to achieve it?

A FEDERAL EXPRESS EXAMPLE: ON-TIME DEPARTURE

BACKGROUND

After eight years as a senior manager at Federal Express, my last project was to build the superhub. This was a $100 million project to take the company from a capacity of 80,000 packages a day to 800,000 packages a day and more. Because the main part of the sort could only take two hours, this amounted to going from 40,000 packages an hour to 400,000 packages an hour.

One of the most critical goals of the hub was 100% on-time departure for all of the airplanes. If the plane arrived late at Newark Airport, the trucks would run into significant traffic, and costs would skyrocket while service suffered. Multiply just this one market times all the other cities, and we calculated that, for every minute we were late with all the airplanes, the cost was $10,000!

PROBLEM

After three years and $100 million in very sophisticated package-handling and sorting systems, we still had less than 50% on-time departure. It was killing our service and our overall costs although the hub costs alone came down.

We had tried everything that we could think of. We put in a countdown clock to provide minute-by-minute feedback to the 1,200 people who worked in the sort. We tracked performance daily and had meeting after meeting to resolve the problem with little progress. We got into the high 50s, but were still well shy of our goal.

SYSTEMIC CAUSE

We hired a behavioral consultant to diagnose the problem from a people-behavior perspective. He donned a sweatshirt and worked in the hub in various functions for a week. He also reviewed our compensation system.

After a couple of weeks, he came back with what he believed to be the systemic cause—again lack of relevance.

Because the sort lasted for an intense 4 hours and most of the operation was just 2 hours, we hired part-time people (mostly students) and guaranteed at least 2 hours of pay.

Although the average was 3.5 hours, this was comprised of lots of people working a couple of hours and lots working 5 or 6 hours.

The consultant claimed that, although people liked working for the company, they were motivated to take as long as possible to work the sort. The later the sort went down meant the more money they made.

He suggested raising the guarantee to 3.5 hours. This, he claimed, would have the opposite effect. If they got done in 3.2 hours, they just earned an hourly raise because they would be paid for 3.5 hours and go home in 3.2.

Hub management argued that this would add significant cost to the operation because it would raise the overall average to nearly 5 hours per person. Weighing that possibility against the cost of late departures, we decided to go to the 3.5-hour guarantee.

RESULTS

Within three months, on-time departures rose to over 95%, and field costs went down as predicted. Nearly as important, within six months, the hub operators had worked out a way to bring the average pay level down to 3.5 hours, and the cost per package was back in line.

POSTSCRIPT

It is so easy to put in policies and to take other actions that sub-optimize the total system. This is just one example where cost consciousness at a local level got in the way of the company meeting its obligation to customers in service and cost.

Prior to the causal understanding, blame was being placed inappropriately on the hub management rather than looking for the systemic cause.

The relevant goal of the company was on-time departures at projected costs. The relevant goal of the frontline people was to make as much money as they could. These goals were clearly out of alignment until we changed the compensation system.

Throughout the book, we will provide other examples that focus on the six system attributes. These feedback/relevance issues were used here to underline the tremendous power of cultural structures to influence people's day-to-day actions.

UPS and Federal Express have a clear vision with solid values and are quite good at making goals clear and at providing good feedback. They are also good at looking for systemic causes to problems as is shown in these examples.

Most companies we have worked with are much weaker in these other areas, such as goal clarity and feedback. Each will be viewed in more detail with examples.

Another point…

One might imagine in the pickup and delivery business that you hit a point where you can no longer continue to grow and evolve. You can't drive trucks faster, fly planes faster, get it there any quicker, and so forth, but just the opposite is true.

Individual drivers can learn tricks of delivery, like the driver who times stoplights in Utica, NY, and is able to deliver a package to a retail store before the light changes. There is the driver in New York who times elevators to stop as he walks up to them to go down.

More important, CustomerCulture systems get every employee working on adding value constantly. Therefore, drivers focus on what they are seeing and their personal relationships with customers. Information systems people look for better information systems for customers and employees.

The point is that there is no end to evolution—either individually or organizationally.

By the time Federal Express and UPS perfect their total system, we will be beaming packages or flying them to Mars or finding a totally automated way to sort and deliver packages to the customer.

3

VISION

A goal of any organization is to build an organizational culture that continually evolves to deliver greater and greater value to its customers over time, which leads to greater and greater sales and profits over time.

In order to build a vision of ever-increasing value to customers, some understanding of human nature and what the customers' needs are must be addressed.

Figure 3–1 presents one approach to that definition. On the left side of the chart is value—those products and services that the customer perceives as valuable and is willing to pay for.

Along the bottom is experience. This includes the customers' perception of their experience with your company. Customers can generally define both physical and informational needs. However, most people cannot tell you what motivates them emotionally or spiritually in ways that enable you to deliver the

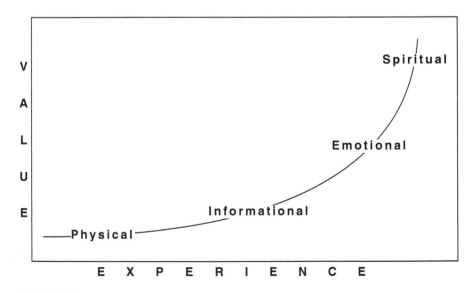

FIGURE 3–1
Customer value-added chart.

experience. They can tell you to what extent they find the experience relatively positive.

For example, people will pay a premium for a brand based on their perception of its value. They know it's the best, but could not tell you why. Generally, this means the company is meeting emotional and/or spiritual needs.

Although companies can define and handle higher level needs, they cannot build the necessary trust by skipping past a need category. For example, I will not trust you to meet my emotional needs unless you've shown me that you can meet my basic needs (physical and informational) first. As a result, you are generally advised to work on one at a time.

Often, leaders talk about value-added activities and adding value to customers, but lack the foundation of value understanding. When each need is met by more than one company, the products and services that meet those needs become commodities driven solely by price.

The company that does not move up the curve gets forced into an efficiency-only mode of operation driven by cost in order to compete effectively. On the other hand, not all companies have products and services that meet higher level needs, but most do if you view the customer experience as the primary focus.

THE FIRST NEED OF PEOPLE IS TO HAVE THEIR PHYSICAL NEEDS MET

At Federal Express, that means getting your package delivered on time. In the beginning, Federal Express was the only company that could accomplish that, but we realized that it wouldn't be long before UPS and others would duplicate the hub concept.

The air hub was the only way a transport company could reliably deliver throughout the United States overnight.

It wasn't long before several companies established their own hub operations and began delivering reliably overnight. As UPS, Airborne, the USPS, and others began hub operations, Federal Express was still able to charge a 20% premium because it had moved up the scale to deliver on the intellectual needs, and the others hadn't.

The intellectual need of package shippers or receivers is to know where their packages are and when they will be delivered. This is an informational need that is nearly as strong as getting the package there on time.

Nearly every company must, in some way, ensure the physical needs are met before they can move up the scale to higher levels. Physical needs include making it easy and convenient to do business, getting a quality product, being comfortable in the buying or delivery process, and so forth. If product quality is poor, making it easier to return it is good, but it will cover up for poor quality for only so long before the customer tires and goes elsewhere.

This level of customer experience is the level that generally keeps people in the game and deserves great attention. Thoroughly working through the customers' physical needs provides ongoing customer retention even in the face of stiff competition and errors. An inventory of meeting physical needs is best identified by using the Hierarchy of Horrors exercise discussed in Chapter 13.

As I go through this evolutionary process, I'll use three disparate examples to show you that the principles apply to nearly every business. The three include Federal Express; Done Services, a drain cleaning service; and the Lund Dental Practice.

Done Services began business by meeting the needs of people with clogged drains. The physical need was to get the drain cleaned, but the company did not stop there, which I'll explain as I go up the value curve. The owner's vision was "one call and it's Done," and the company lives up to the promise of peace of mind—an emotional need.

Paddi Lund, the dentist, meets physical needs by simply caring for your teeth with quality dental work.

However, meeting physical needs of customers is not enough. If Federal Express remained stuck at the physical plane, it would not be alive today.

UPS could, and did, duplicate getting the package delivered on time, and their system is more efficient for two reasons. First, it manages the pickup and delivery operations better, and, second, it has more density because it delivers more packages, thus lowering the cost per package.

On the physical side of customer needs, these two UPS advantages would seem daunting, but by moving up the value-added curve, Federal Express maintained leadership.

Therefore, Federal Express and others continually evolve their operations to higher and higher levels of customer value.

STAGE TWO IS MEETING INFORMATIONAL NEEDS

At Federal Express, that meant meeting the tracing needs of customers.

In the beginning of the company, we would fly customers in on the jump seat and run feedback sessions to discuss customer needs. We defined the six key ingredients to success in priority order. Get the package there on time was number one.

A close second that was somewhat surprising was "tell us where the package is—even if it's on time." This was surprising because I had come from UPS where customers didn't care as long as the package got there.

The overnight business was entirely different as we soon learned. The overnight business is time-critical, and peace of mind was a very strong need. I'm delivering a presentation at noon and have some options if my presentation doesn't show, but I need to know with certainty that it will or will not show up.

We developed the bar-code tracing system to meet the informational needs. Later that evolved to PowerShip, a terminal to give customers the same information that call center agents had. Today, Federal Express uses Internet Ship, which even emails the recipient that the package is on its way and includes a tracing number for the recipient, giving both shipper and receiver total control. The system can even email that the package has been delivered, which is good for big companies that often have a problem finding the package after it has been delivered to the building.

These are examples of meeting the informational needs of customers.

Done Services also moved up the value-added curve by scheduling technicians into very narrow time slots. We've all experienced telephone hookup, furniture delivery, and other services where we have to be home to receive the service. Most companies tell you that they'll be there in the morning or afternoon. Done is able to tell you within 15 minutes when they'll be there. They often respond the same day, and they tell you that when you call. You have the information you need to know that the problem is handled.

Paddi Lund, the dentist, also moved up the value-added curve. Most dentists assume the customer doesn't need information.

They embark on the work without informing the client what they are doing, or, at best, they inform you while your mouth is open and their hand is in it.

Paddi, on the other hand, has client lounges. After a preliminary examination, he takes you back to your private lounge, brings in tea and fruit, and calmly discusses what needs to be done to provide a healthy mouth. This puts people at ease and makes them far more willing to proceed with the work.

STAGE THREE IS MEETING EMOTIONAL NEEDS

Meeting informational needs often naturally evolves to meeting emotional needs.

Knowing my package is going to be delivered on time gives me peace of mind, which is an emotional need. Knowing my drain will be cleaned and operational by this afternoon gives me peace.

Knowing exactly what needs to be done to promote my dental health and learning that in a peaceful, friendly surrounding gives me peace, and, because all medical work is very personal, makes me want to do business with the person who cares enough to sit down with me and inform me.

The first step in meeting any customer's need, whether physical, informational, or emotional, is to know who your customer is and what the specific needs are.

Interestingly, at Federal Express, it is not necessarily the people who benefit directly from the service, but rather their designates.

For example, an executive who needs something overnight asks his or her assistant to get it there, not really caring how, so the customer is the assistant, not the executive. In addition, the assistant's emotional needs are different than the executive's.

The executive wants the package there when needed and the peace of mind that it will be there. The assistant wants to keep the boss off my back, an entirely different emotional need.

The reader may recall Federal Express commercials where the boss comes storming into the office demanding to know why the package wasn't delivered on time, and an assistant, looking at a terminal, says that the package was, in fact, delivered this morning at 10:13 a.m. and signed for by John Jones. After this, the boss timidly backs out of the office, and the rest of the office people applaud.

Clearly, the commercial made the assistant the hero because she got the boss off her back, and Federal Express gave her the tools to do it.

For a while, most shipping people were treated with more dignity and respect by Federal Express than their own company gave them.

UPS is currently running similar commercials that take place in the shipping department with a young man challenging the old ways because UPS gives him the tools.

UPS also meets emotional needs by washing every truck every night whether it needs it or not. This rather expensive operation has been repeatedly challenged over the years during difficult times, but, as a core company value, has been maintained. The reason is simple, yet deceptive.

People don't see, for the most part, how their packages are handled, so they have no easy way to determine the quality of handling. Neatly uniformed drivers driving clean trucks and efficiently doing their jobs gives people the impression of quality because they can see it.

Done Services meets emotional needs with peace of mind prior to the call, but really drives it home during the service call.

The homeowner's emotional need is to have the peace of mind that, after my drain is cleaned, I won't have to spend the rest of my day cleaning up after the drain cleaning technician. Now, most companies would attempt to deal with this need by talking about it in brochures, advertising, yellow pages, and so forth.

Done Services wanted to convey a much more powerful experience. Drivers carry several uniform changes in their truck so they always show up in a clean, white uniform and driving a clean, white truck.

For a while, they even showed up at the customer's door with a red carpet and a vacuum cleaner rather than drain-cleaning equipment. The technician would go to the problem area and put the red carpet and vacuum cleaner down before getting the drain-cleaning equipment. This shows the homeowners in a very powerful way that their homes are sacred and will be treated with great respect.

When I see a cleanly uniformed technician and a clean truck, I am stuck with the idea that cleanliness is a value and again have the peace of mind.

The red carpet and vacuum statement was so strong that it also created story-telling and word-of-mouth sales.

The important point to be made here is that emotional needs are personal needs and must be delivered by employees who care. Showing up with a red carpet and a vacuum with a surly attitude that is incongruent with the clean theme not only doesn't meet the emotional needs of the customer, but creates an equally powerful opposite reaction because it is incongruent.

The emotional needs of the dental patient are met in literally hundreds of ways mostly invented by the seven people who work in the office with Paddi Lund the owner, not Paddi himself. In

Chapter 13, you will see how these value-added services are created on a continuing basis at the Lund practice.

A few dental business examples...

When you arrive at the practice, you ring a doorbell and are greeted as if you were arriving at a good friend's home for dinner—always by name and often hugged. You are escorted to your own lounge where you are served tea and fruit and where you discuss any dental health issues.

The point is that your emotional needs are met in very personal ways by people who care.

One of the companies that does a great job in meeting its customers' emotional needs is Harley-Davidson. Harley discovered that the emotional need is lifestyle, freedom, and power. It has little or nothing to do with transportation.

The Harley Owners' Group (HOG) was formed to satisfy this need.

Delving more deeply, Harley discovered that noise and vibration gave people the sense of power they wanted emotionally. It is interesting that Japan has had difficulty competing with Harley in its category because Japanese manufacturers' sole purpose is to eliminate what the customer wants emotionally—noise and vibration.

STAGE FOUR IS SPIRITUAL NEEDS

By spiritual needs here, we don't necessarily mean religion although it may mean that to some readers. By spiritual, we mean a greater purpose where people (customers and employees) see that they are part of something greater than themselves.

The highest paid people who do the work in the U.S. culture today are athletes and entertainers. Although this may not sound like meeting spiritual needs, they do take people away from their egos and focus them on something outside themselves.

A winning sports team gives its fans the feeling of relating to something greater than themselves. A good movie gets people away from the humdrum of their lives and, again, makes them part of something greater than themselves.

In the beginning of Federal Express and most start-ups, there is a near-spiritual zeal for the company and its products. At Federal Express, a driver hocked his watch to pay for fuel to finish his deliveries. A pilot used his personal credit card to get the sheriff to let him take off. Six hundred people received a paycheck with a note not to cash it, and very few left. At this point, the company was out of money, but not out of spirit, and people did whatever they could to keep the company going, including forfeiting their own paychecks.

These are just some examples where employees demonstrated a spiritual zeal for their company and its success. Without this zeal, Federal Express would not be here today, because the zeal was picked up by customers who also wanted to be part of something bigger.

At UPS, many of their people are said to have "brown blood."

Done Services grows and attracts employees and customers because it is a company that respects and cares about its people. Its people are paid on performance and make nearly twice the industry average, but, according to its employees, that is only an indication of an owner that cares about the people who help him achieve his goals.

It is values driven and gets ordinary people to rise above the ordinary and do what is necessary to deliver extraordinary service.

Probably the best example of a company meeting spiritual needs is the Lund Dental Practice. The practice does business by invitation only. Clients are able to recommend other clients to the practice, but they are reviewed by the staff and then asked to come into the office.

The entire focus of the staff and the dentist is on people, particularly the clients, but it extends into personal lives as well. It is clear that certain spiritual principles are at work. One such principle is that you receive what you give.

It took the better part of 10 years and an incredible focus on going up the value curve to build the business, but it is clearly a model of the future that will ultimately be duplicated in businesses around the world.

In summary, well-designed cultural structures enable a company to move up the value curve continually over time. The value curve is the evolutionary vision that most CustomerCultures have in one way or another.

This does not mean that, after a company has met the core physical needs, it no longer has to be concerned with physical needs. Quite the contrary, a company and its employees must continually reexamine how well they're meeting these needs with a never-ending vigil.

The key to moving up the value curve is to engage every employee in the process of growing as individuals and as an organization, and that requires cultural structures.

A great exercise for building a vision is to write a description of the experience you are attempting to create for your organization. You, as a leader, essentially put yourself into the mind of your customers, employees, and owners and relate the experience of the ideal. This exercise can be done for a company or even for a department in a larger organization.

Appendix A provides an example of such a descriptive experience.

VALUES AS WORDS VERSUS VALUES AS ACTIONS

Values, when practiced by all employees, define a consistent customer experience in action. Values lay out the rules of the game that are being played by employees and observed by customers.

This chapter shows how to define and inculcate customer, employee, and owner-focused values at all levels of the organization.

Values are the noncompromisables that define the organization. They attempt to define what is acceptable and what is not. They are the in-bounds or fair play area of your business world.

A story that comes to mind that demonstrates values in an organization is often told by my friend, Frank Maguire. Frank worked for Kentucky Fried Chicken at the time that it was sold to Hublein, the food giant. Frank worked personally with Colonel Sanders, who had a strong set of values—values that enabled him and his organization to pioneer in the fast food franchising business.

At the time of this story, the Colonel had sold his company, and the new president had taken over. As is often the case, there is a conflict of cultures and of personal management styles during the transition.

One day, Frank was in a meeting of about 30 people, including the new president. The meeting was to evaluate the new company's desire to save money by making the gravy from water rather than milk.

The Colonel saw that there was a meeting and came in uninvited and sat down next to Frank. Immediately he asked, "What're they talk'n 'bout Frank?"

"Colonel, they're thinking about making the gravy out of water instead of milk. They've conducted taste tests with more than 300 people, and the customers couldn't tell the difference. They figure it will save about three cents a serving and save hundreds of thousands of dollars."

After hearing this, the Colonel shouted without hesitation, "Don't mess with ma gravy."

The new president saw this as an opportunity to demonstrate who was in charge. "Colonel," he said, "whether you like it or not, we're going to make the gravy out of water. We've done the research. Customers can't tell the difference, and we're in this business to make money, and water gravy will make us more money. End of argument."

Colonel Sanders glared at the new president while tapping his fingers on the desktop. Then, without comment, he got up and bolted for the door.

"Where are you going, Colonel?" the president asked.

"Goin' on the Johnny Carson show. ...Tell 'em this shit ain't fit to eat," he replied over his shoulder as he left the room.

Needless to say, they didn't change the gravy formula, at least then.

This is a good example of values in action. The Colonel didn't spend one second on whether or not it was a good idea to make gravy from water. He spent just a brief time figuring out how to stop the insane breaking of his core value about product quality.

This is the nature of values. Like a football player stepping out of bounds, the only question is whether or not he stepped out, not whether it was OK to step out. If he did, the play is over. There is no debate.

As mentioned, UPS washes every truck every day whether it needs it or not. A core value of UPS is cleanliness. This value is printed in its policy book, but, like all solid values, it is lived in action. In most UPS facilities, you could literally drop a hamburger on the truck floor, pick it up, and eat it without thinking twice.

As a manager, I remember going to operating centers and asking the manager to take me out to his personal car. When he did, I would ask him to open his trunk. If the trunk was filthy and/or unorganized, I would give the manager a speech about the value as lived in his mind. "If you don't live it personally, you really don't believe, value, or live the value. It is not important to you personally if you don't demonstrate it in everything you do, and your people will pick up that it's not important."

Once, I called a long-time friend who was a UPS district manager (local vice president). I asked him what he was doing, and he was sitting in an operating center watching the center manager mop the truck floor by hand.

My friend had arrived, and the center manager had committed a Value Violation by enabling the appearance of his center to become sloppy. To drive the point home, my friend ordered him to get out the mop and bucket and mop it by hand. It took him most of the day, but that was the last time my friend had to make the point.

UPS doesn't call it a Value Violation, but it does enforce its values.

Another of the UPS values is "a fair day's work for a fair day's pay." UPS automatically invited the union wherever it went during its high geographic growth period of the 60s and 70s. When negotiating contracts, it would rarely quibble about hourly pay, but would go to the wall on working conditions that would prevent high performance for that hourly pay.

Its major indicator of success is cost per package. Cost per hour was far less important. UPS would pay more per hour if it could get more packages delivered in an hour—at least enough to offset the increase in cost per hour.

Finally, after decades of measuring performance, it now pays its drivers by the load. UPS may dispatch an 8.5-hour load and pay the driver 8.5 hours for the day. If it takes the driver 7 hours, he or she just got a raise. If the driver wants to take it a bit easier, he or she takes a per-hour pay cut. Either way, the company owners get "a fair day's work for a fair day's pay."

Another UPS value is consistent and reliable service. Rather than measure service as a goal, it looks at it as a value. You must deliver all your packages each and every day. If you cannot, you report it as essentially a Value Violation rather than a measure of success.

Probably the best example of a values-driven company is Larson-Juhl, the leader in the picture-moulding and accessories marketplace. It has six values:

- Customer always comes first
- Fairness and honesty in all dealings
- Respect for the individual
- Excellence in products and service
- Rewards tie to performance
- Leadership by example

What makes Larson-Juhl unique is the company's way of inculcating its values. Its values are far less specific and therefore require interpretation, action, and discussion at all levels in order to be lived. When joining the company, each employee (Larson-Juhl calls them team members) is given a plastic card with the values printed on it.

Often, during the employment interview, the manager interviewing will hand the potential employee the values card, explain the importance of the company's values, and ask the applicant to describe what a particular value means to him or her. This enables the interviewer to determine, to some extent, the cultural fit.

Larson-Juhl has 22 distribution centers with sales, warehousing, and delivery team members. In addition, manufacturing, customer service, and administrative teams participate in the values program so that nearly every employee is involved.

In order to drive the values home, the company offers a Gold Values award to the top three teams each year (Gold, Silver, and Bronze). This is not a trivial award. A typical team might have 15 employees who share a $35,000 prize. Each team member receives a gold medal and the opportunity to select and vote on a local charity to give $15,000 to. Far greater than the financial award is the pride that is instilled in the winning team.

The winning team must demonstrate its rigid adherence to all of the values. The selection process is quite subjective with top company executives visiting the finalists and making their choice based on their interpretation of how well the values are being lived.

Various team leaders applied all kinds of techniques to win the award. In one center, they got enough cars and excitement to take all employees to visit the last year's winner to discuss what the winning team members did and duplicate their experience. There are some very interesting stories of team members getting together and envisioning that they won the Gold Values award.

In one case, team members were asked to envision the day of notification. They could hear the phone ring and the excitement in the manager's voice nearly a year before the winning team was selected. During the ensuing year, they often came back to that vision and discussed how well they were doing toward achieving the vision.

In one center, the manager held a values session each week for several months. He would ask employees to pick a value and give several examples of how they lived that value and what it meant to them. Some of the presentations were nothing short of inspiring to all of the team members in their group.

Quality is a key issue for the company. You can imagine a valuable piece of artwork or picture encased in a costly frame with a flaw in the moulding. This was unacceptable in the Larson-Juhl values scheme. One of the warehouse operations was called chops. Customers (frame shops) would order the moulding cut to specification, and the chops section would cut the miter for each of the four frame pieces.

The cut had to be precisely measured and cut to perfection. Even a slight splinter would spoil the final appearance. Achieving this level of perfection was a very difficult challenge. Order entry had to get the order precisely right, the warehouse had to pick the right moulding, the saw operator had to make the cut absolutely accurate, and the final packaging and delivery had to complete the transaction—all with absolute perfection.

In one of the warehousing teams, every team member had two jobs. One was the job the team member was hired to do, and one was to add extra value to the operation.

For example, a warehouse person whose job was to fill orders might have the job of heading a committee on waste removal. One of the team members who worked in the moulding chops department in this center was in charge of the quality committee—a core value team.

The committee met each week and applied the normal quality-circle techniques and got the quality to a reasonable level, but not good enough for its quality chairman. He wanted perfection. He went back in time, on his own time, to look at his quality day by day for a year.

He was attending college at night and noticed that when he had an exam, his quality suffered. As a result, he began to tell his inspector to be extra careful on days when he had an exam that night.

He learned a very interesting truth. When he was aware of the problem enough to tell his inspector, his quality went up even on days with the exam. Just the awareness and expression of a potential problem corrected the problem. He found that, as he expressed his concern about quality, he was more focused and careful than he would normally be.

Paddi Lund's eight-person dental practice also developed a strong set of values. Paddi calls these values the Courtesy System. These are eight values that are directed at having people work together congruently. They are simple, but profound, values when carried out.

For example, when you want something from another, say please. When you get it, say thank you. Never talk about someone who is not present unless you speak as if that person was present and use his or her name in every sentence.

Although these are simple values that work well in any workgroup, it is very interesting to go into a workgroup that is not using them and observe the behavior. Chapter 15 discusses this value system in more detail.

At Federal Express, the values were expressed as People, Service, Profit with core values coming out of each piece of this core philosophy.

For example, on the People value, a Guarantee of Fair Treatment (GFT) policy and process was developed. Basically, this said that employees had the right to be heard if they felt they were treated unfairly in any way.

A no-layoff policy was developed and has been followed even in very hard times by the company. This basically said that People were more important than, at least, short-term Profits. Profits would not be gained at the expense of the employees. In the beginning when the volume wasn't there, pilots would work in the hub, sell, and even manage stations rather than be furloughed.

So, the development and inculcating of values is the second step in building the success structure. Values simply communicate the sense of principles and rules that the corporate leader would instill if he or she was present in every operation. Values, as vision, generally reflect the values of the organization's leader. These two tasks in building the success structure (vision and values) cannot be delegated.

5

GOALS

There are libraries of books written about goals and their importance for both individuals and organizations. Goals are used in this chapter in the context of fitting into the overall cultural structure. Goals provide focus and direction for people, but, without relevance and feedback, become just numbers on paper. The cultural structure suggested in this book provides a framework for determining the nature of goals and for setting and achieving goals.

In this context, goals have several attributes:

- The goals are balanced. The purpose of a business is to serve people, although business leaders sometimes focus on the signposts (numbers) rather than reality (people). The people served are the customers, employees, and owners. All are important in developing the goal categories.

  Many companies focus primarily on goals for the owners (stockholders). This makes sense. If an organization could have only one goal, stockholder value sums up all that the company has to offer in one number—share price. However, the purpose of goals here is to focus people on activities that increase value to customers. Considering that purpose, shareholder value tells only a very small, and mostly irrelevant, part of the overall motivational picture.

- The goals must relate to the overall goal of sustained, profitable growth. Sustained means long-term, employee-oriented goals. Profitable means short-term, owner-oriented goals. Growth means mid-term, customer-oriented goals.

- Everyone knows the goals. Goals understood only by the leaders of an organization are achieved only by dictating actions. The objective of the customer cultural structure is to have everyone, customers and employees, focused on doing what is necessary to achieve the goals of the organization.

- The goals are measurable. In order for the cultural structure to work, people must see goals as relevant and must receive feedback on how they are achieving the goals. Without measurability, feedback becomes primarily judgmental and subjective and based on the personal whims of the boss.

■ There should only be three to five goals. This applies to the company as a whole. Each workgroup's goals may be different, but the goals support the organization's goals. A person can relate to only a few things well at any given time. As a result, the goals must be relatively few. My experience is that when there is only one goal, it is understood very well, but misses the need for balance.

Taking these five attributes, we'll set up a framework for goal categories.

Customer goals provide the anchor for goal establishment.

Customer goals generally consist of two categories: promised vs. actual (objective goals) and customer experience (subjective goals), although the bottom line for most organizations is sales. If sales are doing well, customers are buying, which means they are relatively happy with the value that the company offers.

The problem with sales as a bottom-line goal is that it can be driven by factors well outside customer value, such as the economic situation, how well the salesforce executes, and so on.

One example of a customer-specific approach to goals is the Federal Express Service Quality Index (SQI).

The SQI is a very sophisticated customer-oriented goal. The SQI was established by looking at what can go wrong (see Hierarchy of Horrors in Chapter 13) and assigning point values to the frequency.

For example, the worst thing you can do to shippers or receivers is to lose or damage their packages. A lost or damaged package receives 10 points. The least mistake you can make is to deliver right-day late. The package is delivered on the right day, but didn't arrive by the promised time. This event receives only 1 point.

The points are multiplied by the frequency and added up daily, and the goal is to reduce these overall points, even in the face of increasing revenues and packages.

The SQI, like all solid cultural structure elements, evolved over time from a simple beginning. The initial customer goals were packages and service level. Packages were a solid indicator of customer acceptance, and service level was an indicator of how well the company met its customer commitment of getting the package there on time.

As the company matured, its customer goal got more sophisticated with the SQI. This is not dissimilar to the Dow Jones average or other indicators of success that place values and summarize using one key indicator.

At the Lund Dental Practice, the customer goal was quite simple. How many of the customers who visited the practice today will refer a friend? This goal was measured by employee perception daily and was very effective and quite long term in its implications. It gradually led to deciding which customers it wanted referred to the practice.

Many highly successful businesses are very specific about the types of customers they want to serve and the value they bring to those specific customers. As a result, the Lund Dental Practice focused on the Referral Index as a way to differentiate the customers it wanted to serve and to deliver extraordinary service specifically targeted at those people.

For example, the Lund Dental Practice decided that it wanted generally happy people who were into dental health as opposed to people who didn't care about their health in general or their dental health specifically. As a result of its customer-oriented goals, the practice gradually grouped its customers and focused on delivering great service to its "A" customers and literally getting rid of its "C" and "D" customers.

This point cannot be overemphasized. All too often, companies view quantity of customers as all important and leave quality of customers out completely. As Paddi Lund says, "When you try to be all things to all customers, you are often perceived as nothing to no one."

There appear to be two types of goal thinking: top line and bottom line. The point here is that both are important. Yes, healthy organizations grow in sales (top line), and healthy companies are also profitable (bottom line).

This type of thinking is often accomplished through pricing structures that ensure profitability.

For example, if you drop off a package to a Federal Express drop-box, you receive a discount. Although the low-volume shippers are normally not very profitable, they become profitable because Federal Express lowers the cost of the transaction by getting you to drop off the package and avoids the pickup costs that are much more expensive than the discount.

Another way to implement a profitable customer measure is to develop a customer sample and measure its loyalty over time through repurchase rate, customer surveys, and so forth.

Employee goals are more difficult to set and manage.

Many business leaders do not see employee happiness as a goal of the enterprise. They do see employee satisfaction, reduced turnover, employee dedication, and productivity as worthwhile goals—all of which relate to employee happiness.

The real goal is to have passionate employees who deliver extraordinary service to their customers, either internal or external, and who are constantly finding better ways to deliver more value at less cost to those customers.

The challenge is that this is difficult to define and to measure.

At Federal Express, the employee-oriented goal of the Leadership Index is the primary indicator of success in building a strong and productive workforce. Once a year, employees complete a 26-question survey that evaluates their perception of the company as a whole.

The first 10 survey questions are focused on leadership and how well the company, their workgroup, and they are led in their perception. Statements like "I am well informed" are responded to on a scale of 1 to 7.

As Fred Smith often said: "You measure a manager's management ability by evaluating the results of their workgroup. You measure their leadership ability by asking the people they lead." This survey is clearly not a popularity contest, but rather asks the types of questions that bring out the employee's perception of the company and its leadership practices.

At the Lund Dental Practice, each day employees were asked to rate their relative happiness that day on a scale of 1 to 10. One employee called it the stress-o-meter because they learned, over time, that happiness and productivity were inversely proportional to workplace stress.

The practice's goal was to have an honest 8 to 10 achievement against that goal. I say honest because people naturally want to be perceived as happy and are inclined to over-rate their happiness when in the presence of others. It took months for people to realize that, as they admitted their unhappiness, they were able to resolve its source and therefore increase their happiness.

Other employee-oriented goals include reduced turnover, employee productivity, and so forth.

Owner goals are more traditional and are easily measured.

Stock price for public companies, earnings per share, revenues, profits, productivity, and so forth are typically understood and applied in nearly all large companies and many small companies.

It is suggested here that whatever owner goals are selected are publicized for all to see in a place where any employee has access. The Internet provides a convenient place for goals and their status to be published.

The overall idea is to pick one or two goals each for customers, employees, and owners, which, if met, will enable the company to continue to grow profitably (sustained, profitable growth). These become the corporate goals. Then each department, division, or organizational group picks three to five goals that enable it to do its part in meeting the corporate goals.

The best way to determine if a given company is living its goals is to go to the front line and ask employees what the company's goals are.

I suspect that, if you did this in most companies, you would find that their employees don't have the vaguest idea of their organization's goals. This obvious lack of awareness by the people who are tasked with meeting the goals is why companies don't meet their goals as often as they'd like to.

A good example of integrating this three-constituent approach (customers, employees, and owners) is the Federal Express People-Service-Profit value system. Goals are set for the People (employees), Service (customers), and Profit (owners) parts of the business.

Goals are set for each with the results posted:

- People: Employee Survey and Leadership Index conducted and posted annually.
- Customers: Package count and SQI posted daily.
- Owners: Cost per package and profitability calculated and posted weekly.

Another example of goal integration is the Lund Dental Practice. Goals include Customer Referrals, Employee Happiness, and

Revenue Production, which are all reviewed in a 10-minute meeting each day.

UPS, during its transition from retail to what it described as wholesale (business to business and consumer package delivery), is a good example of strong goal establishment and execution, but unbalanced.

During this high-growth period in the 60s, the company was very clear that it wanted to deliver better service at less cost than its only real competitor at the time—the USPS. UPS also wanted to make it profitable.

Its primary goal was cost per package. Its service goals were exceptions (packages not delivered) measured daily and weekly. These goals were measured and reported daily and weekly in each local operation. Incredible focus was placed locally (each local building and the district), regionally, and nationally.

At the corporate level, UPS had revenue growth and profitability goals. Each quarter, these goals were represented in the stock price that was set by the board of directors according to a formula with judgment applied (at this point, UPS was privately held).

This cultural structure was incredibly successful with the stock price going up nearly every quarter and stock owned by the managers of the company.

The lack of balance was the lack of an employee goal. People were paid well and turnover was very low, but the company was unionized. Union disputes were frequent and ongoing in many of the company's locations.

A Survey Action Feedback program and other projects were inaugurated with success, but the ongoing disputes continued and, to some extent, continue to this day.

Instead of corporate-wide, continuing focus on the importance of people, the company tended to solve customer and people problems in an ad-hoc way.

This may not be true today, but it was true in its transition stage.

I believe that the labor disputes continue to this day because inherent in the company's culture is a we/they cultural structure and employee/customer goals (to some extent) are secondary to owner goals. Hourly people did not get the same advantages or incentives that supervisory people received in stock ownership.

The customer/employee goals, as in many companies, receive 80% of the talk and, at best, 20% of the action. As Fred Smith once said: "You can tell if a company is people centered if its CEO spends at least 50% of his or her time on people issues."

Summarizing, clear and consistent goals are essential to provide direction for each employee in the context of customer, employee, and owner focus, and the next two chapters discuss the relevance and feedback systems. Goals need to be limited, measurable, and communicated constantly so that all employees relate what they do to achieving the corporate goals.

In order for goals to be met, they must be personally relevant to the people who must meet them, and that is the subject of the next chapter.

RELEVANCE

Goals are accomplished to the extent people are committed to accomplishing them. To the extent that people find the goals relevant to them personally, they will do whatever is required and within their power to meet them.

If the goals are not as relevant to the action players, all innovation and direction must come from top management where there may be little visibility to customers or awareness of customer needs.

It sounds simple. Of course, goals must be relevant. However, management all too often assumes relevance based on a limited view from the top. In fact, in most cases, the people who do the work aren't even aware of the company's goals, much less find them relevant.

As with goals, much has been said and tried with regard to compensation and other relevance systems. The purpose here is to put relevance in the context of the cultural system solely to motivate people (meet employee goals) in synch with the customer and owner goals.

UPS, during its high-growth phase, had the best system to motivate the managers in its business, and because it promoted from within, it was a relevance system available for anyone in the company. UPS gave stock, not stock options, but company ownership. It made managers into owners, and every stockholder received the annual reports.

UPS has always focused on productivity as the key company goal. This was measured in cost per package at the manager level and meeting standard at the driver level. Today, UPS pays its drivers according to the work dispatched (meeting standard). More specifically, if a driver is dispatched with X stops, Y packages, and Z miles, based on the specific route, he or she will be paid for the amount of hours required to handle that mix of work.

It took UPS decades to perfect its standards system to the point that the union bought in, but it works today. This also provides more freedom for the driver. If the drivers want to work and think harder, they earn a raise and get 8.5 hours worth of work and pay done in 7 hours.

On the other hand, if they want to take it easy and pace themselves, they can do it in 9 hours. They still get paid 8.5 times their hourly pay rate.

Now, this type of system can be very self-defeating and suboptimizing unless very well thought out. For example, in the 50s, as part of its department store delivery division called retail, UPS, attempting to provide relevance around productivity, gave drivers five cents a package in addition to their hourly pay.

It was a simple piece-rate pay scheme and, at first, it seemed to work very well. Productivity went through the roof.

After some time, however, department store customers began to complain. These customers would visit the department store, make their purchases, and have them delivered to their door. Customers would ride the bus from their apartment and didn't want the hassle of carrying packages home on public transportation.

Like all good relevance systems, when the goals are clear and relevant, people will do what is necessary to meet them, often at the expense of another beneficiary. In these examples, the customer also benefits with high-quality work at the best possible cost.

A few drivers learned that they could pay doormen two cents a package to take all the packages for an apartment building. Instead of making 20 or 30 deliveries to individual apartments, they delivered all to one person—the doorman. This saved enormous time, and productivity jumped. It didn't take long to spread the word, and soon every driver was employing this highly productive solution.

After receiving the packages, the doorman would notify the recipients, and they would come get their packages or pick them up on their way in at night. Back then, customers wanted delivery because they didn't want to carry packages. They wanted them delivered to their door, not to a doorman, so they complained, and UPS dropped the suboptimizing system.

Under the present pay-per-load system, this same danger is present, but UPS thought it through this time and had already put into place some very strong service standards that must be met in order to get paid for work performed.

It is interesting to see how well the clear expression of goals, and the actions that make those goals relevant, enable employees who cannot be supervised directly to perform at exceptionally high levels.

Although this story is 50 years old, the balance of productivity and quality is still equally important today.

Another example is an industry that is just emerging into a Performance Pay System™ and that is the heating and cooling industry.

This is a similar industry to delivery in the sense that its technicians work away from the office, and it is difficult and time consuming to properly supervise their work. Additionally, it is an industry driven by many small companies that do not have the management systems in place to manage these people.

Several heating and cooling companies have implemented a system using flat-rate pricing similar to the pricing system implemented in the automotive industry.

For example, when you take your car to most automobile dealers to get new brakes, the dealer will enter the work to be done, and the time to get it done (flat rate) will be in a database. The dealers charge you that flat rate and pay their mechanics for the flat rate hours as well.

This same type of database is available for the heating and cooling contractor that may be repairing your home heating and cooling system. What has been missing is an ability to monitor the quality of the work. Technology is currently available that enables the contractor to test a home to scientifically determine whether or not the technician's work met the quality standards.

This type of relevance system rewards high-performing technicians and gradually eliminates the less-productive people. This is exactly what the UPS system does as well.

As most managers recognize, business is complex enough these days without having to manage every action and effort that employees take. Pay by the hour means employees earn more by taking more time, which puts employee goals in direct conflict with owner and customer goals. I believe most industries have begun to move away from this destructive goal conflict.

After a solid relevance system is in place, actions will reflect efforts that meet both the owner's goal and the employee's goal while maintaining the quality necessary to keep the customer coming back.

A few examples…

I was riding with a UPS driver in New York City delivering to a large office building. As we got on the elevator, the driver pressed the elevator buttons for the top floor and the floor we were going to. As we got off the elevator, he pressed the down button outside the elevator.

At the first stop I watched this, but didn't ask. We made our delivery and as we returned to the elevator, the doors parted like the Red Sea, so we didn't miss a step or wait for a down elevator.

He had it timed perfectly. After we got off, the elevator would go up to the top floor, receive a down signal, and return to our floor.

In another case, I was riding with a driver in downtown Utica, NY. He would come to a stoplight, press the brake, grab a package, make a delivery, and come back just before the light turned green.

This driver had a goal to rise to the top of the company. This is another major part of relevance. UPS promotes from within. It hires young people with a certain profile and then develops them as managers and executives. This provides enormous relevance for people with ambition, but not necessarily with the education required in most companies.

Given a combination of pay-for-performance and the driver's desire to be promoted to increasingly higher levels in the organization, people get very innovative within their scope of activity.

These are the types of actions driven by clear goals and relevance. Most people are smart and, left to their own devices, will find better and better ways to serve their customers, peers, and owners successfully.

Manager attention makes goals relevant. If the manager continues to talk about customer and people goals, but his or her questions continue to revolve around how many sales the employee is making, sales (owner goals) become more relevant than customers or people.

"Give a person a sense of control over their own destiny and they will do anything you ask." This comment came from Federal Express founder Fred Smith. All too often, company leaders espouse all the right things and then take actions that change the relevance equation or, to put it another way, wrest control from the employee and give the power solely to management.

For example, one top manager observes people and their performance, but, instead of coaching for performance and going through a methodical process for getting rid of poor performers, he simply fires them without warning, often somewhat arbitrarily.

Whether he is right or wrong about his observations and evaluations was immaterial to the company's relevance systems.

People generally make up their own minds about management actions and, if they perceive the action was arbitrary and not based on objective reality, they learn to take actions that are safe and noncreative. Over time, the organization becomes stagnant because hanging on to their jobs becomes more relevant than finding better ways to serve customers and owners.

As a result of this negative relevance system that is often driven by egos rather than sound business sense, Federal Express employed two policies to give employees more control over their own destiny: No Layoff and Guarantee of Fair Treatment (GFT).

Most company leaders want to improve productivity by automating repetitive functions or by simply finding more productive solutions using the technology available. To do that properly, they need their employees' support either to find more productive ways of performing the task with better tools or to support company automation projects.

In this case, improved productivity is the relevant goal. Then, when the productivity enhancements work, they lay off the people. It only takes one of these scenarios for the employees to read the real relevance system at work here. "Support improved productivity solutions and lose your job." Therefore, people fight building better ways of serving their customers, and, more often than not, they fight them covertly as in the Federal Express hub example given earlier.

Seeing this relevance issue clearly, Fred Smith began the company with a no-layoff policy.

In the beginning, pilots would work in the hub, hit the street as salespeople, or work as station managers to avoid layoffs caused by lower package counts. Although layoffs would have been an easy way out, Fred stubbornly held to the relevance principle.

At that time, GET THE PACKAGES was the vision and the goal. Laying off people would deliver a strong relevance message that cost control was more important than company growth (package count) and the employee value of control over their own destiny.

As part of its continual evolution of customer-focused technology, the company implemented its PowerShip system where highly profitable, high-volume customers received a terminal that enabled them to create their own airbills, schedule pickups, and trace their packages. This technology, later followed by InternetShip, eliminated the need for 1,200 people who entered customer airbills into the computer and people who answered the phone, scheduled pickups, and traced packages.

Again, it would have been easy to lay these people off and send a message to the rest of the people that automation meant loss of job. Instead the company developed a rather sophisticated system of placing these people throughout the organization. Many of them were put in a special services group to handle customer issues with the new technology.

Nearly all of these people that might have faced layoffs in most companies found themselves in better jobs.

What was the end result? It was a company full of people constantly looking for better and better ways to serve their customers and a company that constantly employs new technology to maintain its edge in the marketplace.

The second major relevance policy implemented at Federal Express was the GFT.

Fred realized that, in order for the company to grow, it would have to place people in management positions before they were ready and that often people, when they have new-found power, abuse that control. The result would be management actions taken without rational cause and that people could be at the whim of their supervisor and therefore lose control over their destiny.

The GFT policy specifies a grievance process for any employee at any level who believes they have been treated unfairly. UPS had the same type of policy only it was dictated by the union's grievance policy and available only to union employees.

There are specific steps that employees and their managers must take in the process. For example, the employee must talk to his or her supervisor first about the issue before going any further. Then, there are several levels, ending with a jury of peers making the final decision.

At Federal Express, GFT is essential to give people a sense of control over their own destiny, and, for this reason, it is robustly adhered to, even though some employees have used the policy frivolously. The principle is an important part of the Federal Express culture.

Positive relevance actions tie reward directly to performance, and more covert relevance actions give people a sense of control so that they are free to pursue achieving organizational goals without personal or team penalty.

Relevance goes far beyond pay. People are obviously motivated by several actions that can be taken by management, of which compensation is only one. It is the most visible and objective, so some time has been given to its discussion.

Follow-up or feedback is a significant part of making goals relevant.

In a recent example in the heating and cooling industry, service technicians were "spiffed" $25 to talk to their customers about having a diagnostic conducted for their home when warranted. The technicians had a simple and objective test they could conduct that took about five minutes and enabled them to say with confidence that the test was in the customers' best interest.

After several weeks and meeting with the technicians, each of these technicians produced only one lead. The process was explained to them in simple terms. "For a simple service call, you make about $20, and it takes you an hour. Add five minutes, and you can make another $25."

Technicians fought the system in the beginning because the diagnostic technology was used after they completed the work, and, if their work didn't resolve the issues, they would be held accountable and have to go back a second time. This worked for the customer, but was in conflict with the technicians' immediate goals of getting in and getting out.

A follow-up system was implemented to make the system part of the daily routine. The invoice that was also a service ticket left behind after the work was completed was reprinted to include the five-minute test, whether or not the technician conducted the test and entered the reading, and whether or not the technician then recommended the more complete diagnostic.

These new invoices were then reviewed each day by the service manager, and, when the technician did not comply with the new process, it was discussed.

This type of feedback and follow-up is often necessary to get people to implement new practices, particularly practices that are perceived as immediately detrimental. Leaders must make the importance of the new process clear to the employee, get employee feedback as to what it will take to make it habitual, and implement the relevance systems to ensure compliance.

At worst, new procedures may mean some employees have to leave before the new becomes habitual.

Some more simple relevance practices include congratulating an employee for great work or celebrating each success for the team or an individual.

A great technique used in many companies is to hang a bell in a prominent place and ring it when something eventful occurs. This provides a simple, but quite effective, way of routinely celebrating successes and the people who are responsible.

Many organizations use an employee of the month type program to make goals relevant. This certainly makes meeting the goals visible, but tends to make one person the hero while many of the rest of the team see it as something they can't readily accomplish. I prefer a system where everyone who exceeds goals or performs a notable action is rewarded.

An example here is the Federal Express bravo-zulu system where any extraordinary act is rewarded with a letter from the chairman and a $25 bond.

Another example is where one of Larson-Juhl's general managers sat down with each employee at the beginning of the year and worked out a special gift if the goals were met for the year. The special gift might be a golf club or some other personal gift. Money often doesn't work because it goes to pay routine bills instead of being a true reward. At the end of the year, if the employee and team met their goals, the general manager personally went out and purchased the special gifts and handed them out at their Christmas party.

YOU GET WHAT YOU RECOGNIZE

If you recognize what you don't want, you make that relevant to your employees. If you look for and recognize what you do want, you get more of it.

Most management styles tend to look for the exceptions and correct them. The assumption is that, if 95% of what is going on is good, all you have to do is to catch the 5% that is not what you like and focus people on it. Those 5% behaviors will then be corrected.

The only problem is then your attention goes to what you don't want, and you get more of it.

I was making that point one night to a friend who was a kindergarten teacher, and he agreed. "In fact," he said, "if you want concrete evidence of that principle, I'll give you proof." I asked what he meant, and he invited me to his class to experience the results of "you get what you recognize."

I had some time that week, so I met him at his class. After introducing me to a room full of five-year-olds, he asked me to step aside with him, and he would demonstrate his point. As we talked, a little boy got off the floor and began moving toward one of his friends. My friend told him to sit back down, which he did, but then another did the same thing.

After a few more admonishments, more and more children were moving around. It wasn't long before it was clearly getting out of hand.

My friend then said "watch this," and he went over to a little girl who was engaged in drawing something. He knelt down and admired her work with great relish. He asked her what she was drawing, and she explained it to him. Then, he went over to another boy who had not moved and did the same. And then another.

It wasn't long before his class had settled down, and all the kids were back in their area drawing and well behaved.

He came back to me and reiterated my point. "You get what you recognize," he said. "Did you notice how when I admonished the behavior I didn't want, I got more of it and vice versa?"

I was stunned as I watched the children all quietly going about their work.

Now one might argue that adults are different, but, after 40 years in business, I don't buy that argument. I believe adults behave exactly the same way. They simply don't express it quite as openly or as quickly as I experienced in the classroom that day.

INVENTION OF THE EAGLE CARD

We were working with a software company in Dallas, TX, where I made the point about getting what you recognize to a team of frontline people during our weekly "Hierarchy of Horrors" resolution meeting. The team decided to take it on and invent ways of recognizing people for what they wanted.

It created an "EAGLE" card (see Figure 6–1). This was a simple thank-you card about twice the size of a business card. On one side was "THANK YOU" with several lines for the person to write a brief note. On the other side were the words "Thank You For Great Service" and then the acronym spelled out:

E: You EMPOWERED me as a customer

A: You ACCEPTED full responsibility

G: You GAVE what you promised

L: You LISTENED and responded

E: You ENJOY what you are doing.

You are an EAGLE!

The culture we were creating was then called an EAGLE culture where everyone mimicked the EAGLE. The EAGLE con-

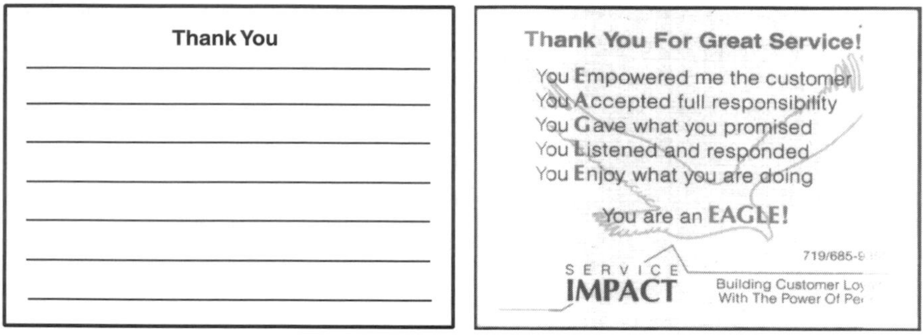

FIGURE 6–1
EAGLE card.

stantly looks for the opportunity. If he or she takes a risk and it doesn't work, the eagle goes back up soaring and looking for the next opportunity.

The EAGLE cards were printed, and each week each person on the team agreed to hand out at least two cards to people who delivered good service to them.

I remember my first card. We were eating at a Japanese restaurant the first night after we had gotten the cards. While waiting for dinner, the bartender was particularly engaging, and I wrote out an EAGLE card and handed it to him. He looked at the brief note I had written and smiled. He said, "You know, I appreciate this more than a tip. It's difficult to explain what it's like to serve people night after night. Yes, you get tips, but that's not what I like about this job. I like people, and I like to serve them. This simple thank you is so rewarding."

Every week we got similar stories from our team members who were engaged in the process. One woman was waiting in line at her bank when she observed how incredible the teller was serving the people in her line. She decided to write her an EAGLE card and, for some reason, put it in an envelope. When her turn came, she slid the envelope under the bars and the teller, not knowing what was in the envelope, pushed the alarm button thinking that it could be an attempted robbery.

Most of the stories were quite touching. One man had given an EAGLE card at a Chinese restaurant. The waitress was clearly Chinese, and she accepted it without any expression and went back to the kitchen. Almost immediately she came running out of the kitchen and said "hug, hug." The man stood up and gave her a hug wondering what was going on. Then, he realized that she did not read English and went back to the kitchen and had the note translated.

We then began using EAGLE cards wherever we went as a consulting team with the same results. Employees in our client companies had EAGLE cards on their personal bulletin boards. Employees began kidding one another as to how many EAGLE cards they had accumulated.

As I personally gave out the cards, I began to see how acutely aware of service I became. I also saw what a joy it was to acknowledge great service and how people, after receiving an EAGLE card, went out of their way to serve. As we discussed these experiences at our weekly meetings, nearly everyone had the same reaction.

They also commented that, as they began looking for and recognizing extraordinary service, they began giving it as well because it was the little things that created the extraordinary experience. After you became conscious of what it was like to receive good service, you began to give it as well.

The EAGLE cards make the goal of serving customers relevant. Nearly every one of our clients continued the use of EAGLE cards long after our consulting engagement was completed. It is a great way to raise peoples' awareness of service and to make the service goal relevant to your people.

There are nearly as many ways of making goals relevant as there are people in the organization. Suffice to say, relevance systems that are in alignment with company goals give people the strong perception that meeting the goals is essential to the company, are very relevant to each person, and are the types of relevance systems that work in building your CustomerCulture.

LEGENDARY STORIES ENCOURAGE LEGENDARY BEHAVIORS

Whenever you attend a seminar about customer service, you are likely to hear some great stories about extraordinary service. A few examples...

There is the Nordstrom tire story. A customer returned a set of tires to Nordstrom, and it took them back and gave a full refund. This is not surprising until you learn that Nordstrom doesn't carry tires.

Or, the time a man was on his way to Wisconsin to play golf with a CEO client. En route, the client called and said that, instead of golf, he needed to meet with the board of directors that afternoon.

The man had no formal clothing. He called Nordstrom to see if it could somehow resolve the problem. When he landed in Chicago, he was met at his arrival gate by a Nordstrom representative. The representative had already scoped out the departure gate and had a complete outfit ready to go. The business man stopped in at the men's room and made his change.

Or, the Federal Express courier who rented a helicopter to deliver a part to a mountain site in the middle of a snowstorm.

The point is that stories do as much to create relevance as anything a company can do. Stories express behaviors that are either desired or not desired, but they tell people what is acceptable or not in an organization.

I started my career at UPS as a salesman. In the early days, when selling the UPS service, you started at the top of an organization and tried to convince the CEO of at least small-to-medium distribution companies that UPS was the solution to its distribution problems. The problem with seeing CEOs, as every salesman knows, is getting through receptionists or assistant screeners who are paid to protect their boss from unwanted salesmen.

The UPS vision was determined people can accomplish anything. If you didn't get what you wanted, you simply weren't determined, and stories often demonstrated in more detail exactly what determination meant.

I'll never forget the stories that began to spread about how to get in to see the president.

A salesman in Philadelphia had repeatedly been rejected by the receptionist of a medium-sized company. Finally, out of total desperation, he asked the receptionist where the guy's office was. Jokingly, she said that he was on the fourth floor and had a fire escape. It was midsummer and before widespread air conditioning.

The salesman climbed up four levels of fire escape stairs and, instead of knocking, simply threw his briefcase through the open window, totally startling the president. He quickly introduced himself and said this was the only way he could think of to get past the receptionist. After recovering from the shock, the president laughed and listened as the salesman convinced him to begin using UPS.

A good friend of mine (the same guy who went to bars to hire drivers at Federal Express in the beginning; see Chapter 1) had the same problem. He had been working on getting to see CEOs in Texas, and the CEO of a major garment manufacturer had continually eluded him. After hearing the Philadelphia story, he decided to try something different.

He was in New York and picked up the phone and called the CEO person to person, collect. He got right through because the outside telephone operator told the receptionist that the president had a collect call from New York (the heart of the garment industry). The president, thinking he had an important customer calling, took the call.

"Hi, my name is Walt Lindenfelser from UPS," my friend introduced himself.

The president was incredulous. "You mean you're a salesman calling me person to person, collect, to sell me something?"

Walt told him that was the only way he seemed to be able to get through. The guy laughed and heard Walt's story and soon became a major witness and customer for UPS in Texas.

About the same time, two of us were selling in Rhode Island. We had the same problem getting in to see the president of a major electronics distributor. We were in the lobby of the customer company and asked for the president. The receptionist said he was in a board meeting. We asked where the meeting was, and she pointed to a door. Without further conversation, we knocked and walked right into the boardroom.

The board members were sitting with very serious looks on their faces, and my partner introduced us and said we needed to see the president on a very urgent matter that would affect his company. The president just wanted to get us out of there and agreed to a meeting, which we later had with him. Although he was visibly upset, he said he admired our tenacity and agreed to try our service.

Later, at Federal Express, we learned to institutionalize the legendary stories. We developed a system to encourage legendary behavior done for the right reasons, gather the stories, spread them, and provide a simple reward for delivering great service.

One courier had a package at Christmas that was wet. She decided to open the package and found it was a sweatshirt wrapped around a bottle of wine that had broken. She took it upon herself to call the shipper and suggest a solution. She then took the sweatshirt home that night, laundered it, picked up a new bottle of wine, packaged it all, and delivered it the next day.

There are literally thousands of stories about this kind of legendary personal caring for Federal Express customers today. These types of stories do not happen because top management mandates good service. They happen because people naturally care and want to be liked and to deliver great service, and...

They work in a culture that appreciates people who care.

After leaving Federal Express, I had reason to be talking to the president of a major insurance company. He mentioned that he was totally loyal to Federal Express. When I inquired why, he said, "doggy bones."

He went on to say how he and his wife spend several winter months in the South. They are both CEOs of large companies and receive urgent letters each day from UPS, the USPS, and Federal Express.

"We have two dogs," he said. "They are very gentle dogs, but make lots of noise, often scaring people. The way that the USPS driver handles them is to pull out his mace. He has never used it, but has often threatened. Our children are grown up. These dogs are our children. Would you use mace on kids if they ran up to your truck?," he asked.

With some kids, I might, I thought to myself as I listened.

"Well, our Federal Express courier takes a different approach. She gives them doggy bones. They can't wait for her arrival each day. To make the story even better, we eventually had a pen built for our dogs. Now she goes over to the pen each day to give them their reward for being her friend."

Again, these types of stories are the millions of small acts of kindness that add up to millions of stories and loyal customers over time.

Summarizing relevance, the question that must be continually asked is this:

Do management actions make goals relevant to the people who must achieve them, or do they send an opposite message, making the goals irrelevant or relevant not to achieve? Do you pay attention to, recognize, and reward the behaviors you want, or do you recognize the behaviors you want to eliminate?

As far as next steps go, implement these ideas:

Capture and spread legendary stories. I have not yet been in a company where they don't exist. People just naturally deliver extraordinary service at times. All you need to do is capture the stories and spread them around the organization.

Implement the EAGLE card program. This program will make people vitally conscious of what it feels like to both give and receive extraordinary service, and it doesn't cost anything. Remember, the bartender said it was better than a tip, so you can save money.

At this point, the CustomerCulture is moving toward completion:

- You have a clear vision that gives people an overall sense of direction.

- People are clear about the values that are important within the culture.

■ Goals are balanced and clear to the people best able to meet them.

■ These goals are relevant to the people who must meet them.

There are two missing ingredients to the CustomerCulture stew. People have a need to know how they're performing against the goals, and then actions have to be taken to achieve the goals.

The following chapter deals with the issue of letting people know how they're doing compared to the company's goals.

You Can't Manage or Innovate What You Can't Measure

I would like to say feedback is the most important of the big three ingredients for success in building cultural structures (goals, relevance, and feedback), but all three are equally important. If there are no clear and balanced goals, feedback is irrelevant. If the goals are not relevant, feedback is ignored.

Like making steel, soup, or any other compound, without all the ingredients in their proper proportion, the result is not complete.

At the beginning of Federal Express, Roger Frock, then general manager, implemented a simple, but very powerful, feedback system. Wherever there were employees, there was a whiteboard, and each morning it displayed four numbers from the previous day's activity (see Figure 7–1).

This was the board in Atlanta that first day (see Chapter 1). After the first day, there was one overwhelming vision, GET THE

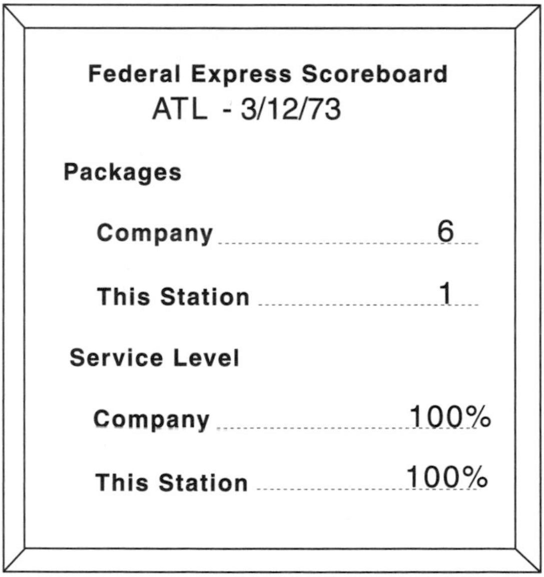

Federal Express Scoreboard
ATL - 3/12/73

Packages

    Company 6

    This Station 1

Service Level

    Company 100%

    This Station 100%

FIGURE 7–1
Early Federal Express feedback board.

PACKAGES, and the feedback system was essential to getting all employees to rally around that flag.

Today, the scoreboard is more complex, but the concept is the same. Let all employees see how they are doing as a team and where practical, as individuals, to achieve the company's primary goals.

Again, it is like a football game where everyone (fans, players, and coaches) is vitally aware of the current results and change their actions according to the feedback they are receiving.

Using the football analogy, feedback is not limited to a scoreboard. Feedback from the coach is constant and often quite personal.

To see is to move. When people truly see the nature of what is compared to what they desire, they will move to correct the situation in ways that are unknown to senior managers. There are examples given in Chapter 1 such as a Federal Express driver who "stole" packages from competitors, a woman who chartered an airplane, or a driver who left his watch with a service station attendant to purchase enough fuel to complete his deliveries.

These examples and thousands more illustrate the actions people will take when there are vision and values, the goals are clear and relevant, and the feedback is simple and consistent.

If my job is to pick up packages, provide great service on the phone, or fly the airplane, it doesn't matter as long as the cultural structure is in place and driven by leadership.

Both Federal Express and UPS use a weekly add-a-line report for weekly feedback. This is a tool that can be used in nearly every industry and is a highly effective weekly scoreboard. Figure 7–2 shows an example of a growth report.

This is a simple spreadsheet laid out for a quarter. The actual sheet shows 13 weeks and has total, percent of quarter, and goal

Fourth Quarter

Weekly Contractor Life Cycle Report		1	2	3	4	5	6
Third Quarter	**W/E**	**6-Oct**	**13-Oct**	**20-Oct**	**27-Oct**	**3-Nov**	**10-Nov**
Customer Awareness - Steve							
Total Leads in System	PLN	-	-	113	-	-	-
# of contractors added to the list	ACT	-	-	4	-	-	-
Total Leads Produced This Week	PLN	-	13	33	75	45	57
Combination of Sales and Marketing Leads	ACT	26	-	4	3	16	-
Leads Produced by Marketing	PLN	-	-	20	20	20	20
# of contractors added to the list	ACT	-	-	4	3	3	-
Customer Acquisition - Al							
Leads Produced by Sales	PLN	-	13	13	55	25	37
Leads produced by sales rep	ACT	26	0	0	0	13	0
Contractors Qualified	PLN	20	40	42	36	28	26
Contractors agreeing to attend meeting	ACT	5	6	15	45	22	-
Contractor Meetings	PLN	11	21	11	15	33	25
Contractors committed to meeting this wk	ACT	5	12	4	12	41	-
Contractors Enrolled	PLN	4	3	3	5	10	9
# fully completed enrollment form	ACT	2	2	3	-	5	-
Customer Success - MikeD							
Contractors Joined	PLN	-	-	-	-	-	-
No. who agreed to join after certification	ACT	-	-	-	4	-	-
Contractors Active	PLN	-	-	-	-	-	-
No. who purchased and are in 4-week period	ACT	-	-	-	-	-	-
Contractor Success Index	PLN	-	-	-	-	-	-
Avg contractor rating based on sampling	ACT	-	-	-	-	-	-
Agreements Closing Percent	PLN	-	-	-	-	-	-
Percent of signups to attendees	ACT	-	-	-	-	-	-
Special focus - Sales							
HW Sales Relationships	PLN	-	10	13	10	10	10
# with ongoing working relationship	ACT	-	10	11	7	2	-
Distributor Relationships	PLN						
# with working relationship	ACT						
	PLN						
	ACT						

FIGURE 7–2
Weekly add-a-line report.

columns. For example, if the quarter is three weeks old (24% of 13 weeks) and the actual is at 24%, the goals are being met for the quarter.

This particular add-a-line report is focused on growth for a small start-up company's growth team (see the concentric organization in Chapter 12) representing marketing (Customer Awareness), Sales (Customer Acquisition), and Service (Customer

Success). Each of these categories of activities represents a segment in the customer life cycle.

There are several things to note with this feedback system.

First, there are only a few critical elements in each of the categories: that the goals of the customer (Customer Success Index) and the goals of the owners (Contractors Enrolled) are shown and monitored weekly.

Employee goals are also included because commissions and bonuses are paid by meeting the goals shown. As the company grows, employee goals will become more specific.

Second, the system is weekly and quarterly, not monthly. At Federal Express, like many companies today, fiscal months are used with months being 4 weeks, 4 weeks, and 5 weeks (or 5, 4, 4), making up a 13-week quarter.

Weeks and quarters are used for a number of reasons.

First of all, weeks are consistent and habitual. Nearly every week is the same, whereas months end on different days, have a differing number of days, and so forth.

Generally, there are meetings weekly where feedback can be used to drive discussion (additional feedback). There are always weekends, and generally people do certain things on certain days. The more habitual a cultural structure is means the more power it has for relating cause to effect.

Second, quarters make a good planning point. At the end of each quarter, people can take a slightly longer view and plan for the next quarter.

Third, the purpose of feedback in this report and all management reporting is to motivate people to act if the goals are not being met or to continue to do what is working if the goals are being met.

Monthly is simply too late to take responsible actions (response-able). If there is too much time between action and result, it breaks the cause-effect relationship and therefore doesn't drive appropriate and timely actions. The actions and the corresponding results don't relate to each other and therefore don't motivate people to act in productive ways.

For example, if I launch a new method of contacting customers this week and don't see the results for 45 days, I will not relate my action this week to results reported in the distant future. On the other hand, if I take action this week and see the results immediately, I am likely to continue the action if it worked and do something else if it didn't.

Of course, there are actions that take weeks and sometimes months to show results, and those results show up on this report as well in terms of expectations.

The point is that feedback needs to be as related to the actions as soon as possible within limits.

The fourth point to make is that, for every success indicator, there is a Plan (PLN) and Actual (ACT) indicator. The idea is to have each person set their goals for each of the indicators they are responsible for and to have them roll up into the company goals.

The best method of doing this is to set the corporate goal first and then work with the team to have its goals match or exceed the corporate goal. In the example shown in Figure 7–2, the corporate goal is five new sales per week with four salespeople. Each person thinks through his or her quarter and sets his or her plan for each indicator. If they don't add up to five, the manager works with them until a reasonable plan is developed.

At Federal Express, this weekly add-a-line report actually became a weekly profit-and-loss report and was balanced every month against the fiscal month's profit-and-loss report done primarily for accounting purposes. The company got quite good at providing a reasonably accurate weekly profit-and-loss statement given certain monthly and semimonthly charges that had to be allocated to a weekly reporting system (utilities, rent, payroll, and so forth).

In the beginning there were three primary indicators of success: package count, service level, and weeks-to-breakeven (WTB). WTB was primarily used by the executive committee to determine if the company was on track for its initial goal of profitability and therefore sustainability.

WTB was calculated each week by taking a simple least-squares distribution and projecting it out statistically to a future breakeven point. In the beginning, at Federal Express, breakeven was more than 100 weeks off, but it kept coming down. This type of indictor is especially beneficial for a start-up because it gives people a light at the end of the tunnel for the struggle that nearly all start-ups go through.

It also tells management when it needs to do something different.

If, for example, based on last week's results, the number of WTB was not at least one week less than last week, the company was falling behind. If the WTB was less than expected, management needed to evaluate what was happening and do more of whatever caused the decrease.

Like any feedback system, the daily and weekly indicators must be given relevance. This starts by making every employee aware of the key company goals, making those goals relevant, and then providing daily and weekly feedback.

After those systems are in place, what really gets and keeps people focused on the goals are management inquiries. If managers pay no attention to the feedback, no one else will either.

In the example used at UPS in Chapter 2, managers began asking questions, and people got really focused on lowering the cost per package. This was not because the goals were not clear or because of lack of feedback, but because management made the feedback and the goals relevant by asking questions.

Implementing good feedback systems is always a struggle. Most managers have their own style and their own timing. A manager who grew up in a monthly system will have difficulty moving to a weekly orientation. Managers who grew up with little or no attention paid to customer and employee goals will have a difficult time balancing their focus on owner goals to include customers and employees.

I am currently going through this, as I am implementing the cultural structure in a start-up situation with managers from varying previous experiences.

The most effective way of converting to a weekly system is to have scheduled weekly meetings, whether by conference call or face to face. During these meetings, the weekly operations report (add-a-line) becomes the primary focus of the meeting.

Because my current company is a virtual company with most of the growth team members scattered throughout the country, we conduct our meeting by conference call each Monday.

We use an agenda meeting style with a facilitator who does not make judgments, but runs the process of the meeting. The meeting has a time limit of one hour, which is strictly adhered to with some exceptions.

The facilitator starts the meeting by collecting agenda items from each participant along with the time that person feels they need to ask, give, or discuss. The one agenda item that is covered first is last week's results from the weekly operating report.

We use WebEx (a technology that enables the facilitator to show information on everyone's screen). Each salesperson states his or her numbers for the previous week, and the facilitator enters the numbers into the report. After each person has gone, management reviews the total and discusses actions needed.

Then, the meeting goes to other agenda items that are brought up at the beginning of the meeting.

This is a highly effective weekly feedback system that consists of the numeric indicators along with free and open discussion.

In the UPS example and later at Federal Express, I conducted these calls daily and weekly because both companies are in the daily business of pickup and delivery, which is mainly a daily business.

For most companies, a weekly system stubbornly adhered to works best for continual and ongoing feedback.

A Good Example Where Feedback Has Been Lost Is the U.S. Healthcare System

In the beginning of the Clinton administration, the Clintons had a great vision of affordable healthcare for everyone.

They did not take a systemic or cultural structure approach to the problem, and therefore little was accomplished. They tried to understand the problem, find its solution, and pass a government mandate to implement the solution. This is typical of most businesses when confronted with a need to move to a new vision or to make a major change in direction.

The company leader states the vision or goal and then attempts to dictate a plan to achieve the vision or to meet the goal.

In the early 1970s, another federal administration had a similar change in vision. The energy crisis and pollution scare hit simultaneously, and the government had to do something about both issues. Instead of taking the Clinton healthcare approach, it simply established the vision and laid out the goals, made them relevant, and mandated feedback.

For example, "By 1995, cars with more than X pollutants will not be sold in America. Beginning immediately, miles per gallon standards will be established for each model automobile and posted on the new car's window."

These kinds of government policy mandates stimulate the related industries to take massive and productive actions. We are far more fuel efficient and less polluting today than we were 40 years ago because the federal government understood and applied the cultural structures approach.

In contrast, the Clinton administration sought to implement a solution rather than to mandate a result, making it relevant and providing or demanding feedback.

If we look at the systemic issues behind the healthcare system, the primary culprit is lack of direct feedback between the provider and the patient. This is primarily caused by a third-party payer system. The patient receives the services and has the provider (physician, hospital, and so forth) turn in the bill, and it is paid by a third party.

If there is poor service rendered or a mistake made in billing, it is irrelevant to the provider because there is no direct feedback from the patient.

I'll provide a couple of examples.

A close friend, an independent business woman, was pregnant. She had decided not to buy insurance coverage on herself, but did cover the baby's delivery because there can be very expensive problems at childbirth.

The baby was born prematurely and a bill for over $20,000 was paid by the insurance company without challenge by either my friend or the insurance company. On the other hand, my friend had a $1,500 bill that was challenged in several ways.

The hospital had charged her for a milk pump. Because she already had one for her previous child, she refused to take it. The hospital tried to charge her for a milking consultant. She had never seen the consultant, so she turned it down. By the time she was done, she paid only half of what the original bill invoiced.

Federal Express, realizing this phenomenon, provides a 40% rebate for all incorrectly charged medical expenses that their employees find on their medical statements. This simple incentive provides direct feedback to the provider from the patient and reduces the overall cost of medical services to Federal Express.

I remember, as a child, riding with my grandmother, who was a doctor making house calls. She had an excellent and very functional relationship with her patients. The feedback system worked very well. This was just after the Depression, and many people couldn't pay immediately or paid in trade. At any rate, the cost of medical care was far less, primarily because the feedback system was operational.

Back to Clinton's vision. Had the administration specified the goals to the three primary institutional players (providers, employers, and insurance companies) and set up the feedback systems, the industry could have or still can resolve the escalating costs of healthcare. I don't mean to oversimplify, but a well-thought-out systems approach demanding solutions from the industry will work.

By attempting to tell the healthcare industry how to solve its problem, the administration ran into unconquerable resistance, which was what happened under the Clinton plan.

More specifically, government might mandate the cost per patient with a time to reach that goal and a relevance factor that would severely penalize the industry. I realize that healthcare cost is a very complex issue and there are no simple solutions, but one thing is certain. The problems in the industry cannot be solved by government.

The people who must solve these kinds of problems are the players themselves, but they must be given the goals, made relevant with feedback to have the necessary determination to solve them together. The only real issue is that the three major players must be made to work together to resolve the issue.

Organizations make the same mistake of mandating actions rather than making goals clear and relevant and providing feedback. CustomerCulture companies then let the players take the necessary actions to resolve the issues.

Similar to relevance, feedback can and must take many forms.

Paddi Lund's feedback system involved daily staff meetings where revenue, customer passion, and employee happiness were reviewed. People then provided feedback to each other during the meeting. During the daily routine, the courtesy system was used, which provided minute-by-minute feedback between all team members.

Objective feedback can be built into the culture with good technology and discipline. Subjective feedback coming from the coach or manager and from peers is more difficult. I find daily meetings using the courtesy system to be a good method.

Our team meets by phone every day, and each person rates themselves on a two-dimensional (2D) scale:

- Productivity on a scale of 1 to 5
- Happiness on a scale of 1 to 5

As long as I am objective, this feedback system uncovers any hidden agendas and puts all the cards on the table for both the manager and the employees.

Summarizing, feedback systems are essential to building high-performing cultural structures, and they cover the objectively measurable along with the subjective judgments of a well-disciplined coach, who provides feedback as close to the point of action in time as possible.

8

EXTRAORDINARY SERVICE IS DELIVERED BY ITS CREATORS

The CustomerCulture is now in place. Your frontline people can articulate the vision of the company. They have a good idea of the values and rules of the game. The goals are clear and relevant. People receive feedback on how they are doing against their goals.

Now, you're ready to capitalize on the CustomerCulture. You're ready to get your people fired up about serving their customers, and the way to do that is let them do it.

At this point, most senior managers bring employees to meetings and expose them to great speakers or launch customer service training meetings, but there is a much simpler answer.

Here's the point. Let your employees invent how they're going to serve their customers.

As one consultant puts it, "The seven most important words in management language are: 'I don't know. What do you think?'"

Here is a case in point.

A Milwaukee hospital CEO had a customer service problem in his emergency department. He had gotten lots of complaints about how long it took to get through it and how people were left waiting for hours. From a business perspective, his census (customer count) was flat, and the emergency department is often an area where hospitals can grow.

The problem became quite apparent when he cut his own hand and went to the department to get it fixed. He was put in a cubicle and asked to wait, and wait he did. However, he wanted to experience his hospital emergency department as a patient did, so he didn't say anything. He just waited and waited.

Three and a half hours later, he finally had someone come in to take care of his problem. Normally, he would have called a meeting with his managers in charge, and he did that, but with a little different twist.

I had spoken at a local CEO meeting, and he decided to try this "let them do it" approach.

The topic of my talk was "Extraordinary Service Is Delivered by Its Creators." The idea is that whoever invents a service concept and process better be the people who deliver it because they're likely to be the only ones who are passionate about it.

I went to Milwaukee and listened carefully as the administrator went through his experience and then asked a lot of questions about the size and organization of the emergency department. I learned that the department consisted of physicians, nurses, and administrators—some 80 people altogether.

I suggested we put together a team of two physicians, four nurses, and four administrators and that team be given the task of reducing the wait time in the emergency department to less than one hour (it was averaging well over three hours at the time). Further, this team should accomplish this feat without spending any money unless it was offset with an expense reduction somewhere else.

The team got together, and my partner, Sandra Judd, and I facilitated a day-and-a-half session with them to invent the solution.

Prior to the session, as might be expected, the ideas to reduce the time centered around adding doctors, nurses, and administrators. When people are not directly involved in the cost structure, their natural solution to any problem is to add resources.

When they realized they couldn't add expense, they turned to using other facilities to create more room, but not enough came out to get people excited and passionate about serving their customers.

These were the general ideas to reduce waiting time prior to our session.

We launched into our invention session, which sought to reduce wait time without spending money.

We usually start this type of invention session with wishes, and we try to get people as wild with their wishing as possible. It quickly became apparent that there were different types of patients. Some were in life-threatening situations, and others had cut their hand and wanted to get back and watch a football game (the administrator's situation).

Realizing this, Sandra gave people different patient roles to play.

"You're a patient that just cut his hand and wants to get back to watch the Packers. You're a patient who just had a heart attack. You're a mother of a three-year-old that just swallowed what you believe to be a poisonous substance. You're the CEO of the hospital who dropped in to have a cut taken care of." And so on.

Then these people began wishing in their roles.

One person wished that the emergency department was like McDonald's. "I wish for a drive-through emergency department. You just hold your hand out, and the person in the window stitches it up."

That got lots of laughs, and the energy in the room increased. Soon there were all kinds of wishes to speed up the process and to reduce the waiting time.

Finally, the heart attack patient said, "Hold on. I wish that you'd take all the time you want. This is my life that we're talking about here."

That got more laughs, and the team was moving. Soon they realized quite clearly that the emergency department needed to be split between two types of patients: the fast track patient and the high priority but slow track patient. They both had entirely different needs. The fast track patient needed quick, efficient handling. The slow track needed testing, deliberate handling, and reassuring and constant communications, including to their loved ones who may be in the waiting area.

After a day and a half, the team had their plan. They would reorganize the emergency department and have a triage nurse (the nurse that does a preliminary diagnosis) send people one way or another depending on their condition and need.

This type of fast track system has been tried and is being used in many different hospitals—some successfully and some not so successfully, but few as successful as in this hospital.

The difference is that the emergency department employees invented it and the details that go with it.

The team set a start date and then went through a very methodical process of presenting the solution first to the hospital senior administrative team and then to the rest of the nurses, physicians, and administrators of the emergency department to get feedback.

These sessions were also facilitated. There was excellent support from the nurses and administrators, but the physicians didn't show up to the scheduled feedback meetings, which were set up to have all emergency department employees attend at different times during the day and night. This type of feedback system is designed to let every employee participate in the changes that affect them.

The fact that some physicians did not attend was not a good sign of acceptance of the new solution, but we assumed that because none of the other physicians showed up, there would be little resistance to the new program. Just the opposite was true.

As it turned out, there was a great deal of resistance from the rest of the physicians who had not been part of the team. These doctors worked for an outside company that provided physician services to the hospital, and they weren't buying it.

We called a special meeting with the physician company and the head nurse and went through our feedback process. We asked each doctor what he or she liked about the new program. Most could come up with one or two things, but there was one doctor who said "Nothing!" the first time around.

After getting many pluses from the other physicians, I said to the doctor once again that there had to be something positive he could say. He blurted out, "At least it's faster for people with minor problems, but..." I stopped him there and said we'll get to the issues in just a moment.

Next, we went through the issues with the new system. This time the opposing doctor came out quickly with his issue. "It seems like we've spent a great deal of time on a drive-through-type process. What about the more serious issues?" he asked. "What are we doing for these people?"

This team of doctors then went to work on that issue, and it was also given back to the original team. The opposing doctor volunteered to lead a small team to deal with the issues more specifically, and the physician resistance was all but gone. His concern about not compromising the quality of care had been heard and dealt with. This subteam, headed by the opposing doctor, even came up with a video information system for the waiting loved ones to keep them informed and to reduce their anxiety to the extent possible.

As the head nurse said, "I don't know how it all happened, but we've got 80 people routing around down there in the emergency department finding ways of speeding the process and better serving our patients—both their physical and their emotional needs and even the needs of the waiting loved ones."

A month later, the team implemented the new process. Thousands of details were taken care of by the team. A month after that, the average waiting time had gone from 3 hours and 7 minutes to 53 minutes and continued to hold fairly consistently.

Part of the plan involved patient feedback about the experience. Again, letting people do it works only when the CustomerCulture system is in place.

We set up a box with happy to sad faces (five in all). The box was about 12 inches long, 3 inches deep, and 10 inches high. The happy faces were placed above a slot where poker chips could be inserted. It was set up at the patient's exit area.

Patients, upon leaving the emergency department, were given a poker chip and asked to place it in the slot opposite the face that best represented their experience. The chips were counted every day, and an index was recorded and posted for feedback.

This type of experiential, noninvasive, and simple feedback system works quite well. The box is on the wall, and people simply go up and insert their chip in a slot below the face. We wanted as emotional (experiential) a response as possible.

At first, prior to the team meeting, the emergency department was rated consistently between two and three. As the team became more and more engrossed in changing the whole emergency department paradigm, the rating began to climb. After implementing the new program, they were getting fours and fives consistently.

This phenomenon has happened dozens of times. When people invent their own way of delivering extraordinary service, it truly becomes extraordinary. The reason for this is that extraordinary service has far more to do with people's desire and power to serve than it does with systems and processes for serving.

Let me say that again. Extraordinary service has far more to do with people's desire and power to serve than it does with systems and processes for serving.

When people truly care about serving others, it shows in the customer's experience.

The process of letting them invent the systems and processes generates both the passion and the process for serving customers efficiently and effectively.

Another reason to have your frontline employees invent their service is that they typically know far more than anyone else, including the customer, about what the customer's needs are. Service experts generally say, "Ask your customer," but the reality is that customers in most situations really don't know what they want—at least not on an emotional level.

For example, if you go to an emergency department at a hospital four or five times in a lifetime, you don't know what you want to experience. You don't think about it. However, people who deal with 100 patients a day know which experiences are received positively and which ones are not. The problem most frontline people have is that they are not given the power or the direction to create the solution.

As the emergency department employees went through this process, they realized they were in healthcare because they wanted to serve, but had built barriers to avoid the pain so often experienced in an emergency department environment. As those barriers built up, they had become cold and uncaring over time.

The process of reinventing service served to make caring conscious and to get many of them to recognize and relive the meaning of providing healthcare.

Stories became rampant. One nurse spent 24 hours straight and the better part of a week with a dying patient even after the patient had been sent upstairs to a regular hospital room. She communicated constantly with the patient's family giving them comfort. By the time the patient died, she was a close friend of the family's.

These stories spread. Some were little things done to comfort or to serve more quickly. Some major actions were taken to make the patient's life or death more meaningful. One of the most effective feedback mechanisms is to spread the positive stories of extraordinary customer experiences and the people who deliver them.

Over the next six months, the census (daily visits to the emergency department) began to steadily rise and went from 92 per day to 133 per day. Hospitals, like any business, depend on continually drawing in patients, and the emergency department is a major gateway. Word-of-mouth spread quickly, and more and more of the community began going to this hospital when they had an emergency.

The bottom line is that extraordinary service is really passionate people serving people. Peoples' natural desire, for the most part, is to be liked and to solve other peoples' problems where they can add value. Our corporate cultures often destroy this natural passion to serve.

That passion is aroused when people are given the opportunity to invent their own version of service. They are close to the customers and know their needs far better than the senior managers of any organization.

With that said, some leaders take this as potential anarchy, and it is anarchy if the company does not implement the goals, relevance, and feedback portions of the overall cultural structure.

Here is another example.

Hershey's Chocolate Company had a problem on its Rollo production line. It had worked with teams of employees to improve quality and had raised the consciousness of their employees around service in all aspects of the operation.

This example involves a problem where the candy went through an automatic wrapping machine, and the wrapped candy was dropped onto a conveyor that dumped it into boxes to be sold in retail stores. When the box reached the specified weight, it would be shifted to a new empty box, and the process would continue.

The problem was that, all too often, empty wrappers would come out of the wrapping machine and end up in the retail boxes. These boxes had cellophane windows where the consumer could see the empty wrappers, and, although the box was sold by weight, the customers' perception was of poor quality and the feeling of being taken advantage of.

The company put a team of engineers on the problem, and a new wrapping machine was not cost justified. Therefore, the problem became "How to get the empty wrappers off the conveyor."

The engineers then designed an elaborate vibratory conveyor system. A vibratory conveyor vibrates, and heavy things tend to move with the force of gravity. In this way, they could vibrate the filled wrappers off the vibratory conveyor to the box filling conveyor. The cost would be about $10,000 to move equipment around and to install the new system. Of greater consequence was the time. This line was working 24 hours a day and 7 days a week and was still falling behind. A retrofit would stall production for a day and one-half.

Fortunately, part of the team inventing the new system was the production workers who worked the line every day. The engineers presented their solution for feedback. The next day, two production workers were discussing the problem just before lunch when one said, "I've got it." The other asked, "What have you got?"

"I'll show you after lunch," came a hasty reply as the man left the building.

After lunch, he returned with a $15 fan he had purchased at Wal-Mart. He plugged in the fan. It blew the empty wrappers off the conveyor, and the problem was solved—no great cost, no stalled production.

This type of story is rampant in companies with a CustomerCulture that truly engages their employees in the process of growing to meet the vision and goals of the company.

The suggested next steps here are to put the CustomerCulture in place, conduct the Hierarchy of Horrors meeting (see Chapter 13), and then let small teams of employees handle the issues. It is important to be very clear about the problem the employees have to solve and the resources that are available.

After the small teams have developed their plan, get feedback from other employees that will be affected by the change. See Chapter 14, "The Seven Dynamics of Change," for this feedback process.

This completes the explanation of the actions to build the structures necessary to establish the CustomerCulture. The following ideas summarize this concept:

- Vision is established to provide general direction.

- Values are defined to give people the rules of the game.

- Goals provide specific direction for the company, its teams, and individuals.

- Relevance makes the goals important to the people who must meet them.

- Feedback lets people know where they stand in relation to their goals.

- Actions are then generally taken as a natural course of daily work.

Up to this point, I have discussed the theory with many examples of how CustomerCulture works. The next part, "The Application," provides more examples of CustomerCulture in action both when the structures are functional and when they are dysfunctional.

THE
APPLICATION

II

Part I described the theory behind building a
CustomerCulture and how it was developed.

The purpose of this part is to provide more specific
actions that have been and can be taken to build a
CustomerCulture. It provides the next steps that,
when taken, will move your organization toward
focusing your employees on their customers.

THE PHOENIX DOG PISS THEORY

The first part discussed proactively setting up functional cultural structures. The applications part discusses the various ways these functional structures are applied in business today.

This chapter describes the more typical organization where building a cultural system focused on customers is not on the radar screen and managers do what they do, often driven by culture, but unaware of it.

One such example, the Phoenix Dog Piss Theory, is an example of how cultural structures and peoples' desire to serve often override management prerogatives.

Large companies are notorious for suboptimizing systems with poorly designed and executed cultural structures. To put it another way, they put in incentives (relevance) that provide motivation for employees to turn their back on customers and opportunities that would benefit the company as a whole.

Most readers, if they work for or have worked for a large company, will probably relate to this without a lot of examples.

Very often, frontline and middle management people, closer to the heart of the business, take actions to serve customers despite the interruptions of senior managers that are often protecting their turf. Rather than a well-defined cultural structure, egos attempt to run the organization in ways that are counter-productive to corporate success.

The Phoenix Dog Piss Theory was developed by Steve and some peers, as midlevel executives for a major manufacturer. After nearly three decades of watching reorganization after reorganization occur, Steve and his peers observed one example of suboptimization in action.

As each new management team came to power, they would have to mark their territory as a dog outlines the borders of his power by pissing in strategic places. After experiencing these reorganizations, Steve realized that each new team would mark their territory by killing old or even recently implemented customer programs.

This was a good way for them to demonstrate the power of the new regime. The new broom sweeps clean.

As a result, these programs would crash and burn and fall into the ashes—the graveyard of tried, but failed, customer programs.

After the new regime settled in, customers began complaining about the demise of the old programs, and the new team would devise very similar programs that were brought to life as the Phoenix rising from the ashes. These programs were given different names, but the essence was very similar to the old ones marked as dead.

After decades of frequent reorganizations, Steve noticed what was happening, and it happened nearly every time. As a midlevel manager, he was closer to the customers that were upset each time an old program was killed.

Not wanting to lose customers, he worked with other midlevel managers to develop and implement the Phoenix Dog Piss Theory to protect customers.

The idea was to assist the new management team in very quickly killing the old programs and then equally as quickly getting customers to communicate the need for new ones to take their place. In this way, the new team could mark their power with less interruption to customers.

The Dog Piss Theory worked, and customers remained loyal in the face of each new management change.

Unfortunately, most large companies are too powerful and bureaucratic to give middle managers the power to bypass the dysfunctional cultural structure overtly and to implement sane and customer-centric actions. Middle managers often have to do it covertly.

Interestingly, this same company has old accounting systems that reward administrative people for not making price changes. Where opportunities exist to increase prices and margins, the system can't handle it simply, so people fight with vigor not to change prices, no matter what the opportunity.

Changing anything from the bottom or customer-focused levels is very difficult in this company. It is the opposite of the learning (and growing) organization.

This is very typical in functionally structured organizations where marketing and sales people are requested to meet growth projections while the finance people are requested to guard the bottom line.

Obviously, both are important, but instead of cultural alignment where every employee acts to produce sustained, profitable growth, some employees hurt growth to guard profits while others hurt profits to produce growth.

One could say this provides the necessary checks and balances like our Federal system—Congress, the courts, and the administration guarding each other. The problem in business is that all these checks and balances do is cost overhead, create bureaucracy, and slow down growth. Ideally, every employee is responsible for delivering value to customers, employees, and owners.

A well-functioning cultural structure accomplishes these ends without lumbering bureaucracies that destroy innovation and customer focus.

Let's look at this example company from a CustomerCulture perspective.

Vision was nonexistent, at least at the level of action.

They are a manufacturing company and, as with most manufacturers, continue to have a vision of great products and technology, rather than products focused on customers and their needs.

As the company struggles to keep pace in a changing world, it continues to hang on to past practices, seeing execution, and therefore organization and management, as the core problem. It keeps reorganizing and changing top management hoping that a new team will solve the problem.

There are few perceived values at the level of action.

Growth goals are clear. Meet the quarterly sales goals or else. These goals are singularly focused on owner goals. Customer- and people-oriented goals are not clear if they exist at all. People are rewarded (relevance) for guarding the status quo. As the company moved into the information age, it was ill-prepared to change and to grow and was sold to another company just as ill-prepared to move aggressively into the 21st century.

As an example, the company has recently introduced a periph- eral product in one division that has the potential of dramati- cally benefiting another division in the company. Because the incentives don't reward people in the sponsoring division, man- agers wanted to ignore the potential of the new program.

It was pissing on their territory, and their relevance systems rewarded them for squashing it or at least not working with the benefiting division to the substantial benefit of the whole.

Fortunately, the Dog Piss Theory worked once again, and saner minds prevailed.

Quarterly revenues drive nearly every company, but this com- pany is so driven by its quarterly goals that it moved from an approach that would ensure success by its channel partners to a program that would meet quarterly goals at all costs.

The usual way that manufacturers handle meeting quarterly goals is to push inventory into their channel or pipeline by offer- ing specials and other incentives to purchase at the end of the quarter. Often, this inventory is purchased at a lower price and then forced down to the next level and so on. Some channel partners understand this way of doing business and even wait to the end of the quarter to purchase.

Focus is essential for every company, and quarterly goals with good relevance systems and feedback daily or weekly provide focus. The problem is that most quarterly goals and relevance systems are primarily conceived and implemented by the people at the top with little or no input from the front line. Senior managers assume that they understand in some detail the focus that will bring success.

All too often, it is the people closest to the customer who understand best what will bring success, but are powerless even to suggest goals and relevance that will motivate actions to deliver more productive ways of succeeding.

By implementing balanced goals focused on customer, employee, and owner success and backing those goals with solid relevance and feedback systems, the cultural structure drives every employee to focus on meeting the goals in whatever ways he or she can meet them. As a result, the company changes, grows, and meets changing customer needs as a matter of course.

Fortunately, it's generally the informal structures, such as the Dog Piss Theory, that are the most powerful within organizations.

Managers close to customers are often driven as much or more by unstated customer-oriented goals and relevance systems than by the formal systems. The feedback system employed in this instance will have more to do with customer feedback than with the more formal, numbers-oriented systems used in this example company.

The point is that many companies succeed despite themselves because people want to serve and, in the absence of well-thought-out cultural structures, will find ways to do so.

A regional test was conducted in another major company. The feedback system, or dashboard as it was called in this case, was one-number sales. This single-point focus gave away margins, and, in this limited test, it was costing the company three times the cost of the product to complete the sale for many of the products with an overall average of 34% of the sales price to consummate the sale.

However, lower margins and profitability often don't matter to a top-line-focused company. Sales and market share at all costs was the goal. Market share was the result. This major company was on the rocks with this kind of thinking. The cost of sales was only one symptom of a much greater problem—unbalanced goals.

Then, a new CEO came in and focused on profitable sales.

He discovered that because of misguided relevance systems (commissions), processes were put in place to ensure every salesperson got credit for their customers' orders. As a result, every customer had to track down their salesperson to place an order. Not only was it very expensive, it was very inefficient and troublesome for the customers.

By balancing the goals to include both sales and profits for the sales organization, the people developed more streamlined ordering processes for customers and reduced the direct cost of sales from 34% to 7%.

These are just two examples of dysfunctional cultural systems. These types of examples are rampant in nearly every large company that doesn't proactively develop their cultural structures in a very methodical way.

Overall, goals must be balanced to meet the needs of customers, employees, and owners. Another way to put it is that every employee focuses on those activities that lead to sustained, profitable growth.

Sustainability means focusing on customers.

Profitability means delivering enough value so that the customer pays for profits.

Growth means focusing on sales without compromising customers or owners.

The questions to ask with every new program are these:

- Will this focus people in ways that support sustained, profitable growth?
- Are the goals clear, balanced, and in synch with the vision?
- Are the goals relevant to the action players without suboptimizing the whole?
- Is the feedback clear and simple, and does the feedback create appropriate actions?

If the answers are yes to all, the proposed program has been thought through, and, if the commitment is there, it cannot help but succeed.

BIG COMPANIES ARE LIKE BIG SHIPS—SLOW TO MOVE AND SLOW TO CHANGE

Companies today are living in a world that is fast moving and fast changing.

How does a well-thought-out CustomerCulture make big and bureaucratic companies more nimble in a fast-moving and changing world?

Some ships are highly effective. Take aircraft carriers, for example. They combine the power of the ship with the nimbleness of the airplanes on the deck.

The ship provides the support system for the airplanes. The airplanes provide the nimbleness and ability to engage the enemies where they are.

This is an easy metaphor to understand in channel-dependent companies (those companies that distribute their products through third-party retailers or small companies. This includes most manufacturers). It is also a reasonable metaphor for companies doing business with employee teams, as long as the CustomerCulture is in place.

The big company could be the aircraft carrier seeing its role as providing support for its channel partners, who are close to the customer and who are very nimble at changing with every change in the marketplace. Channel partners, as small businesses, are so nimble that they constantly alter their business as necessary for survival and thrive no matter what the economy throws at them.

This same support/action system can be developed with employee groups, but, for purposes of simplicity, we will concentrate on an example of a major manufacturer that cannot be named and how it is in the process of building the aircraft carrier and the jet airplanes.

This is a company that sells home products and home diagnostic equipment to and through local contractors (channel partners). In this particular industry, although there are 140,000 contractors in the United States, the company is focused only on the top 2% where, working together, it could build a highly effective delivery system that would work for all participants.

Most major companies simply try to fill the pipeline by pushing inventory to the reselling channel partners and leave it up to them to move the products to their customers.

This company decided to take a different approach. Company leaders reasoned that, to the extent the manufacturing company and the contractors could work together, perhaps there was a way to respond to customers in highly creative and productive ways. Now, that said, there is not a company around that doesn't espouse working with its channel partners as partners. The problem is that few do it.

First the company had to come up with enough value to get the channel partner's attention. The company started with expensive home diagnostic equipment ($22,000) that would enable the contractor to diagnose a home's environmental systems thoroughly. These systems use 60% of a home's energy and, when running properly, create a healthy, comfortable, and energy efficient indoor environment.

Many of the contractors did well with this diagnostic technology, and many did not. As a result, the company's product often ended up on the shelf even after a $22,000 commitment.

The diagnostic equipment enables the contractor to define the cause of high energy bills, lack of comfort, and poor indoor air quality.

Working with a pilot contractor group, the company was able to develop a system in which, using the diagnostic equipment, the contractor could identify the causes of home problems and sell the repairs a high percentage of the time.

However, that wasn't enough value. It is a great product, but the company didn't provide the support necessary to ensure contractor success. The jets were on their own without a strong base to come back to when the business wasn't there.

To put it another way, many contractors purchased the equipment, but didn't have the internal support systems to market the new technology to keep the equipment busy diagnosing and selling repairs. Only about 50% of these top contractors were showing success in their mission using the equipment. They were jet airplanes not doing much damage to the enemy.

Then, the company called in marketing, operations, and technology experts, along with several of its contractor partners, and met for a day and a half to brainstorm how they might take the technology and build a business success model together. Most companies see their channel partners as customers to be sold. This was not a typical company-to-channel partner presentation, but rather an all-out, no-holds-barred brainstorming session where people worked as a team focused on the end customer to build a high-performing program that would work for both company and partner.

This team of aircraft carrier executives (company people) and jet airplane pilots (channel partners) reasoned that whoever could get the consumer to respond and provide an ongoing stream of business to the contractors could build a partnership that would benefit the customer, contractor, and company.

These contractors have several frustrations, three of which are relevant here. First their business is seasonal. During extreme weather (hot or cold), they are very busy repairing broken systems. During mild weather, their business dwindles.

Second and relating to the first, their customers call them only when they have a major problem. This leads to new customer acquisition only during very busy periods when the contractor is least able to serve the customer and when the new business is least needed by the contractor.

Finally, most of the contractor businesses are owned by people who started as technicians and, as Michael Gerber puts it, had an entrepreneurial seizure to get into their own business. The problem is that they are the business. They have not built a business that can run without them. They work *in,* not *on,* their business. They are the business and have not systematized enough to build a high-performing machine.

These frustrations provided an opportunity for the company to build systems that could substantially benefit their channel partners and their customers.

After some brainstorming and ensuing development, the team came up with a number of programs that have been implemented throughout the channel network.

One of the programs is called Demand Marketing. The team developed a very compelling homeowner offer directed at a major U.S. problem—indoor air pollution. Without going into a lot of detail, the offer gave peace of mind to homeowners concerned about indoor air pollution. Essentially the offer was...home air quality peace of mind for $50!

The company (aircraft carrier), on behalf of its contractors, sends a simple, plug-in air quality monitor that is tied to the Internet and monitors what is going on in the home with the theme "Your children may be the canaries that test the air quality in your home. Now there is a better way."

If the device discovers a problem with air quality (low humidity, high particle count, high carbon monoxide, or a number of other problems), the company calls the customer and schedules a home diagnostic with the local contractor to determine the cause of the problem.

In effect, this program provides a marketing system for their contractor partners and makes money by helping the contractor acquire new customers during the off season and the carrier company takes a percentage of the initial fee for the home diagnostic performed by the contractor.

The Demand Marketing part of it involves very carefully record-keeping of who responds to what. As Jay Abraham (an entrepreneurial marketing expert) often says, "Test, test, test. Don't be so arrogant as to believe you know what your customers will respond to."

Therefore, the company tested. They tested the offer, the head-lines, the media, the homeowner list, and so forth, and gradually developed a very hard-hitting campaign that essentially took over much of the new customer acquisition function for their channel partners. These partners were great at fixing things and even fairly good at selling things, but had neither the resources nor the expertise to get the phone ringing.

This is the type of value that the aircraft carrier can bring to the jet airplanes. A single contractor couldn't afford the time and resources to set up a system of this kind. However, the company serving thousands of contractors across America can, at close to 1/1000 the expense per contractor.

After the statistics are in, the contractors can dictate the level of business they would like. If they want five diagnostics a week, that means sending out 1,150 postcards to a specific consumer list to get the responses necessary to book the desired diagnostics. This is very important during the off-season times when the contractor needs the business. During the busy season, most want no new work, so they do no Demand Marketing.

In another move to support the airplanes on the deck, the company offers cobranded Web sites to their partners. Professional, high-performing Web sites cost a great deal to develop and maintain. The contractor could afford a brochure Web site, but not a commerce Web site or a Web site that would draw consumers to it from a national brand.

Therefore, the company put in the time and resources necessary to provide a high-quality cobranded Web site, and it got its contractor partners to pay for it.

The real advantage goes back to the aircraft carrier and the jet airplanes. After a mission, the jet pilots come back and debrief. The mission command becomes very familiar with what is happening at the point of engagement and alters or supports the mission with that information.

By cobranding Web sites, the company has a very powerful informational system.

For example, when a specific contractor runs a newspaper ad or a radio commercial on its own, the company is aware of it because the contractor's Web site visits go up. The system then has an easy response mechanism to ask the contractor what it did, get the response, and then offer that information to other contractors in similar but noncompetitive markets.

If a contractor runs a successful newspaper ad in Dallas, the copy can be sent to Atlanta and other similar cities for their use.

The command center of this system is a simple Web-connected personal computer (PC) where a map of the United States is shown with colored dots. The colors represent performance levels for each contractor week by week. By clicking on a dot, the system drills down to the specific partner where the detail is shown. It is like a pilot's cockpit where the instruments are visible along with the ability to communicate immediately with the partner to determine cause.

The colors also represent a major change where that ad run in a Dallas newspaper shows up because the Web site visits went up out of proportion to previous weeks.

When you take the thousands of people who are calling on customers every day and dealing with local markets and combine that with an intelligence system that is constantly gathering information and disseminating what works to others, you begin to build a CustomerCulture that is a quantum leap when compared to competition.

You are constantly innovating to meet customer needs with little or no risk. The risks that are taken are taken locally by astute business people who will live or die depending on their ability to change with changing customer needs.

These smaller businesses must innovate and evolve constantly to remain viable. Their innovation is focused on the customer rather than corporate politics and other ego-protection issues.

The CustomerCulture system simply ties this innovation into a high-performing network using Internet technology to weave that network together.

I am amazed at how few companies have implemented this relatively simple and pay-as-you go program on behalf of their channel partners. Some executives have argued that this type of partnership development is too costly. The cost of the program mentioned was 10 people for two days, including travel, and one person taking the ideas and following through with the program development and execution.

I believe this obvious opportunity and resulting lack of action by channel-dependent company leaders comes back to culture.

Most of these channel-dependent companies view their channel partners as customers, and, in that view, they take a sales posture rather than a partnership posture. Most relevancy is based on how much the company can sell to the customer partner, rather than how successful the partners are with their products and services.

The systemic problem is poor vision, goals, and relevance.

Nearly every company has partner advisory boards, but most are used to stuff more products and services down customers' throats rather than to cocreate a model that will make both entities successful. Aircraft carriers are useless without the jets. Jets would have no place to land without the carrier.

The next major step is to search deep down and be honest about how you see the channel partner (or employee group). If you see them as customers to be sold rather than partners going to market, that mindset must change. If you see your employees as robots to do your bidding, that mindset must change.

The focus of all participants must be on partner and company success—never one at the expense of another. It should be considered one organization of people working together to achieve a common vision and goals, not separate entities each working for their own benefit at the expense of the whole.

Of course, each party, as well as each individual, will look out for his or her own interests first, but, as trust builds, so will the CustomerCulture.

After the mindset is clear, you work with your partners to build a carrier/airplane partnership using the best attributes of both parties dedicated to an end of delivering value to the end-user—the people directly benefiting from the company's products and services.

Techniques such as cobranded Web sites, joint marketing programs, and such will develop as the partnership develops.

The essence of working with channel partners and employee teams is to deliver high-performing systems, systems for delivering increasingly higher and higher value to customers. The next chapter reviews the dangers of oversystematizing.

SYSTEMIZE THE ROUTINE; HUMANIZE THE EXCEPTION

The best time to capture customers is when they have a problem that you can solve. This is true whether it is a new or existing customer, but especially true with an existing customer.

Retailers have known this since the beginning of the last century and have continually offered money back or exchanges and turned themselves upside down if necessary when there is a problem. They know that people talk and spread the word when there is an unresolved problem. They also know that a problem resolved turns an upset customer into a raving fan.

Federal Express has understood this since its formation, and, even in the midst of a major effort to use technology to lower cost by automating the tracing and information functions, the company still enables the frustrated customer to talk with a person.

It is beyond my wildest imagination why so many companies and, in fact, industries ignore this simple principle.

You Can Turn Angry Customers into Raving Fans Simply by Solving Their Problems

Years ago, IBM conducted a study to determine the validity of this principle. It found that if it implemented computer systems correctly and without a major issue, its repurchase rate was 84%. That is, 84% of those customers purchased additional systems when they were necessary.

When the customer had a major problem resolved, the repurchase rate was over 93%.

Given that fact that is intuitive, logical, and validated, entire industries ignore this principle and tend to do things to aggravate angry customers rather than win them over for life. The only reason this works is because very few companies within an industry get out of their box long enough to challenge old practices.

Here are a few examples.

I, as a customer, have a software problem and call the vendor. My system's not working, and I have a deadline. I'm frustrated, angry, and very anxious. With few exceptions, I get put in voice-mail jail while I listen to various options, press a key, listen to various options, press a key, listen to the options, and so forth. You get it.

Then, I finally get to the end of the tree and am told that I have a waiting time of 18 minutes, and then I am periodically told how important I am to the company. This obviously adds to my comfort that the company really cares enough to solve my problem.

It is often said that actions speak louder than words, but voice-mail jail speaks louder than all the marketing in the world. You have to have a great, noncompetitive product to remain in business or at least be in an industry where no one else is any better.

Certainly, software vendors have a problem. If they make it too easy for their consumers to call and get an answer, no one reads the manuals. Therefore, the smart ones charge for and give great service. There is a Microsoft® service, for example, where you pay per call and get fast and excellent service.

In another example, I am at an airport waiting for a flight. It is delayed, and I can see that, but cannot get information. Because I don't have information, I have no options other than to sit around and hope someone will tell me something. Usually, this is another passenger who has heard something. People are frustrated and upset all around me, and some are even screaming at the gate agent to no avail.

Airlines probably have several delays every day for 365 days a year and yet still find it difficult to build the systems to keep their customers informed. Informed customers can make the decisions to call or do whatever to take control over their own destiny.

That's all people really want: Control over their own destiny. Take that away, and you really have an upset customer.

Current technology would make it very easy to send an email or computer-generated call to a customer whose flight is late and save a rushed trip to the airport. Technology could also have the people picking them up automatically notified if a flight is late, saving time on both ends. This is building systems to focus on customer issues that demonstrate that you care enough as an organization to solve their problem.

I spent a couple of hours talking about this one day to an airline gate agent friend of my son's. She initially felt there was nothing she could do. People didn't keep her informed. Then, we did some brainstorming, and she gave it more thought after we parted.

A month and a half later, she won an employee award by scoring the highest of any gate agent in the airline's system that month. Later, she told me the story. She had a flight from San Francisco to Hawaii that was delayed. Instead of fighting with angry customers, she went on the offensive and committed to keep everyone as informed as possible.

First, she got on the microphone and told the customer of the delay and that it would be about 30 minutes. She also committed that she would tell them whatever she knew at least every 10 minutes.

Then, she began joking with them as the delay got longer and longer. She told them at one point that it was a bad part and that a new one was being rushed over. When it didn't come, she told them laughingly that they lied to her, but then, in seriousness, told them that the part didn't fix the problem.

As it turned out, the flight was delayed more than six hours, but with all that, people boarded the flight in a great mood and rated her higher than any gate agent that quarter. That plus her other ratings earned her the award.

I could go on and on about how companies deal with angry customers, but I don't need to. You probably have as many stories as I do about your experience of zero power in a difficult situation and the employees that either had no power or no passion to resolve your issue.

Here's the point.

You systematize what you can, but always leave the customer an out to be able to talk to a human being.

You systemize the routine and humanize the exception.

Airlines could challenge their employees to come up with a process to handle delayed flights. Maybe it's only communication, but it's something that understands the exception to their overall passenger-handling systems.

Software companies could challenge their service people to come up with a way to deal with frustrated customers.

A while back, Federal Express implemented its PowerShip system where high-volume customers received a terminal that enabled them to schedule a pickup, trace a package, send in their billing, print a label, and so forth. When Federal Express did this, all kinds of money was saved by the company. What traditionally was an employee function became a customer function, and the customers loved it because it gave them control.

Federal Express has a no-layoff policy, so the 1,200 people who had jobs that were no longer necessary had to be slotted elsewhere. One of the functions they were placed in was a customer

VIP function. With the new system, daily contact was lost, so they set up a department that could handle the exceptions promptly and completely.

As the company has moved into the Internet era, the same thing is true. You can call on the phone and do most things automatically (systemize the routine), but when you have a problem, hit the button and you are talking with someone. The amazing thing is that, most of the time, representatives have your screen up by the time you hear the voice so they can help you immediately (humanize the exception).

How do you do this? How do you systemize the routine and humanize the exception? I alluded to it earlier. You involve your employees (see Chapter 13).

You challenge your engineers or systems people to systemize the routine, and you challenge your service people to humanize the exception. You tell them they can't spend any money or in fact have to reduce the costs of handling the upset customer. You will be amazed with what they come up with.

In this process, you begin looking at and treating your people as customer problem solvers.

I remember going on a ski trip with Vince Fagan, the senior vice president of marketing at Federal Express in the early days. We had developed a very customer-centered culture, but were growing very fast and losing the culture fast as we hired more and more people to keep up with the growth.

Vince knew how to bring in customers with TV advertising and other consumer marketing techniques, but he didn't know how to keep them coming back—to build customer loyalty for life.

I had just gotten back from learning a problem-solving system called Synectics™. I tried the system with him and we really got bizarre with our ideas. What came out of this airplane problem-solving session was a definition of the Federal Express employees that got people thinking differently about our customers and our employees.

Every employee was a problem solver.

No matter what the job, your job became solving the customer's problem. The customer may have been an internal customer or an external customer. It didn't matter. Your job was to solve the problem. As Fred Smith later put it, "The sun will not set on an unresolved customer or employee problem that is not dealt with in some way."

Fully 90% of what most people and companies do is habitual, yet most people and companies continue not to systemize the routine and often try to systemize the exception.

We have voicemail systems and Internet sites that systemize the exception in attempting to deal with irate customers. We have plane delays that need to be systemized, but become exceptions.

The idea is to create habits for the routine and jolts for the exceptions.

All too often, system designers try to automate functions that must remain human and, in the process, spend far more time and resources on the system while losing customers.

Where there is total automation, the customers should have an out and the ability to talk with a person who can solve their problems when there is an exception.

Several new technologies make this type of systematization possible. Technology makes it possible to identify callers by their telephone numbers. This allows banks and other companies to separate their customers by profit level and offer special services to good customers or customers they want to improve their relationships with.

For example, a high-profile banking customer calls and is routed directly to his or her customer service agent. A catalog company that today makes its customers remember and punch in their agent's extension number can route the call directly to the agent without voicemail. If the agent is busy, the customer gets voicemail, but it is personal, not institutional, voicemail.

Knowing the telephone number can combine products with the customer to avoid the customer having to enter in products or go through the never-ending automated inquiries and responses. For example, if I call in with a Windows Millennium edition (Me) problem, the agent puts that into the record. The next time I call in, a different agent asks if I am still using Me. If not the record is changed.

Another example is the September 11, 2001, terrorist disaster and how it has affected air travel and air security. Instead of building systems to handle the routine, our leaders elected to make every traveler an exception.

What do I mean?

One way of making the exception the routine is to offer frequent travelers the ability to go through a one-time personal history check that they pay for. After this check is complete, a special ID would give them faster clearance through airport security. These people essentially go through a security check first and then go through a streamlined process from then on.

This still might involve bag checks and so on, but not in-depth checks. Then, airport security focuses on the exceptions who are not frequent travelers and are more productive with those people.

This is very similar to air crew security systems where the air crew goes through security with less restriction.

This type of system is used for virtually every security need where industrial or government employees are cleared for various levels of access to buildings and information. Yes, some of these precleared people might become targets for terrorists because they have been cleared, but random inspection would resolve that issue.

Another example of going with systems that need humanization is also the travel industry's response to the September 11 disaster.

An airline in the United Kingdom wanting immediate resolution to falling load factors made the decision to offer a £10 one-way airfare to anywhere in its system. It sold 750,000 tickets in weeks and got its load factor moving. It also probably gained market share in the process and certainly demonstrated a desire not to let the terrorists win.

Compare that "humanizing the exception" action with the U.S. airlines. The government jumped in to bail the airlines out while they cut schedules, laid off people, and generally watched as load factors and the hospitality industry receded.

What would have happened if our government said we will be glad to cover your losses based on load factor? You achieve this load factor, and we'll subsidize you during this transition period. You do whatever you need to do to get Americans flying quickly.

It all goes to cause and effect and action and reaction. You have a goal that is relevant and a feedback system that tells you how you are doing. You give people, industries, and/or companies the goal of getting people back into the air; you have them provide their load factors, which proves they are accomplishing the goal; and then you let them figure out how to get people flying again.

Another great example coming from September 11 is General Motors and its no-interest car purchase offer. Its goal was to get people buying automobiles, and its management immediately saw September 11 as an exception and humanized it. It didn't take long for General Motors' competitors to follow, but, unfortunately for their competitors, the cost of the financing was not built into their product.

General Motors humanized the exception.

Here are the next steps.

Visit your company as a customer and feel your experience. If possible, visit the company when you have a problem or are upset and see how you are handled by your systems and your people.

Then, begin challenging your managers and your people to take a look at where your systems are making your frontline people impotent to solve their customers' problems. Also have them look at where you are spending inordinate amounts of time doing things that should be systematized.

If you use automated voice attendants, challenge your people to come up with a system that truly understands your customers' frustration levels and deals with them.

Perhaps someone will develop a technology to sense just how irate or anxious a customer is and to provide a way of routing the exceptions to a human being that can at least listen.

In the meantime, passionate and determined employees can find solutions to systemizing the routine and humanizing the exceptions.

The following chapter deals with how organizations are structured and how most organizations are structured to focus most of their people on everything but the customer.

THE SINGLE EGG ORGANIZATION

O rganizational structures focus people on corporate objectives and provide relationship structures. The purpose of this chapter is to propose an organizational structure that focuses employees on their customers—whether internal or external customers. It is called the "Single Egg" organization and was invented by employees from a healthcare insurance company. The single egg analogy provides a central focal point—the customer as the yoke of the egg.

So far, 28 different companies, including Federal Express, Larson-Juhl, and even the Paddi Lund dental practice, have already moved to the organizational structure proposed in this book. They have had great success at keeping their people focused on adding value to their customers' experience.

One major paradigm to be challenged is the way that most companies are organized so that the focus is on everything but the customer.

Most companies use a hierarchical organization with the CEO on top, implying that the customer is on the bottom (see Figure 12–1). The problems with this type of structure are simple and obvious. Each vertical box has different goals. Some serve the customer, and some serve other gods, such as fiefdoms,

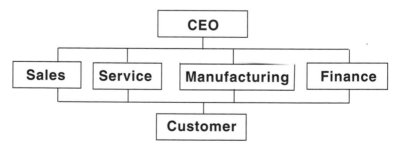

FIGURE 12–1
Typical organization structure.

profit at the expense of sales, sales at the expense of customers and profits, and so on.

The goal of any organization is sustained profitable growth. However, with the traditional organization, different pillars of power focus on a piece of the whole, generally leaving the focus of the company where the most powerful pillar exists.

The sales department focuses on growth, often at the expense of profit. The finance staff focuses on profits, often at the expense of growth, and so on.

The sales organization wants to keep a customer, even if the customer has a questionable ability to pay. Finance wants to fire the customer that doesn't pay. The result is an internal power struggle and a customer who receives mixed signals from the company. Salespeople have nothing to lose and everything to gain by becoming the champion of the poor payer. Conversely, finance has nothing to lose and everything to gain by firing the slow payer.

The company can lose either way because neither sales nor finance has an incentive to deliver increasing customer value that leads to sustained, profitable growth.

The goals of the traditional organization are suboptimized. Each pillar of power has its own goals that relate to only its mission, which is generally focused on everything but the customer and a specific subgoal of the company.

To rectify this obvious inconsistency and, in an attempt to convince employees that the company is customer centered, executive management turns the organization upside down and puts the customer on top (see Figure 12–2).

All you get then is an organization that is upside down and backwards. The fundamental systemic cause of poor customer focus and suboptimized goals is still alive and kicking.

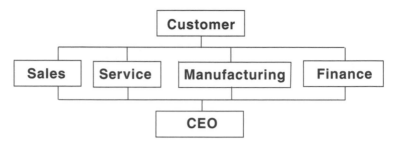

FIGURE 12–2
Typical organization with customers on top.

THE SINGLE EGG ORGANIZATION

Many companies have gone to a customer-centric organization where customers are clearly in the middle of the organization and surrounded by the people who can support them (see Figure 12–3).

Each circle represents a customer to the next circle out. The growth organization serves the outside customer. The fulfillment organization serves the growth organization and so on.

The customer is the center of focus of the entire organization. However, each suborganization has its own customer set.

As mentioned, this organizational structure was invented by a team of frontline people for a healthcare insurance company. The employees were frustrated with their company's inability to serve new customers by setting them up quickly. The landscape had changed.

Where once it was fine with the customer to take 60 days to bring a new customer online, escalating healthcare costs meant companies would change carriers at the last minute and wanted a quick response from potential new insurance carriers.

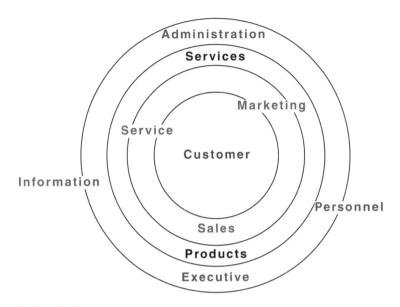

FIGURE 12–3
"Single Egg" organization.

Management formed a team of salespeople, service people, claims processors, and others and gave it the goal of reducing the set-up time to 30 days or less. When the team first met, one of the field salespeople asked where the 30 days came from. In her opinion, 30 days was too long. Ten days made a lot more sense.

This team worked together for a few hours a week for several weeks and came back with what it called the "single egg" concept. The customer was the yoke, and the white of the egg was integrated teams of sales and service people all focused on specific customer and/or geographic groupings.

Serving these teams were claims adjusters. The rest of the company, described as the frying pan, was there to support these two groups. The company implemented its employees' recommendation, and customer ratings and sales began to climb.

The organizational system was then described to many other companies that decided to change their structure to the Single Egg Organization.

Here are a few examples.

Federal Express Creates FedEx Services

A few years back, Federal Express purchased several organizations in order to round out its strategy of becoming the total logistics solution for its customers. It purchased Roadway Package Service (RPS) for ground service, a logistics company, and so forth, to add to its air express service. For years, Federal Express attempted to operate these new organizations as separate entities.

There was a reason to keep the organization separate that had to do with union organization. By merging RPS into Federal Express, the drivers and other package handlers would fall under a different labor regulation and could organize locally instead of nationally.

As separate organizations, the customer who wanted to ship ground by RPS would deal directly with RPS, and the same customer who wanted to ship by air would deal with Federal Express, the air carrier.

There was little opportunity for either the customer or the company to develop a partnership with the customer to resolve their logistics issues.

Additionally, there was no common theme or brand. RPS and Federal Express were two separate organizations owned by FDX, an unknown company.

After a few years of separate operations, Federal Express decided to go to the single egg organization.

In the spring of 2000, the company made a bold move by branding all company entities as Federal Express companies (FedEx Ground, FedEx Express, FedEx Logistics, etc.)

More important, the company established FedEx Services as the customer interface organization. The function of FedEx Services is to work directly with the customer. The traditional functions of marketing, sales, customer service, and all customer interface functions reside in FedEx Services. This new organization has at its disposal all the various services offered by the entire organization.

If a customer needed ground service, air service, or total logistics services, he or she dealt with one organization. This type of structure is a systems approach to customer focus.

The customers of FedEx Services clearly are the people who ship and receive packages by air, ground, special truck, and so forth. They are also the people within the customer organization that plan and execute logistics and distribution strategies.

FedEx Services' job is to bring the full offering of Federal Express to solve customer problems. It learns what is available through the various Federal Express divisions and provides those services to the customer. It is, in effect, the customer of the various operating divisions. For example, FedEx Ground serves FedEx Services by providing ground pickup and delivery where and when they are needed. FedEx Express provides overnight services generally by air.

Using this organizational structure tends to break down the pillars and focus all employees of the company on their specific customers.

This type of structure works well when the rest of the CustomerCulture functions are in place. For example, the goals of

FedEx Services have to include sustained, profitable growth. Otherwise, the organization will tend to focus on the customer and growth at the expense of profit.

LARSON-JUHL COMBINES SALES AND SERVICE LOCALLY

Another company that changed its organizational structure is Larson-Juhl. The company was traditionally organized with 22 branch offices consisting of warehousing and local delivery of its products.

A separate sales organization of 100 salespeople reported up through a sales vice president.

The customer would deal with the sales representative and then the fulfillment function as two separate functions or faces within the company, often at the expense of meeting their objectives.

For example, the salesperson might commit to a time of delivery that was not in the best interest of the delivery function to meet. The delivery people were rewarded for lowering the costs of fulfillment, not meeting the customer's timing needs. On the other hand, the salespeople were rewarded for keeping the customer happy, often at the expense of increasing costs, which would eventually go back to the customer.

The company was slow to change, and focus on the customer was split between sales and service.

Larson-Juhl reorganized into the Single Egg Organization by putting general managers in place in each of its 22 local offices, and these general managers focused on the customer with both sales and service reporting to them locally. Customer needs were identified by the salespeople and fulfilled by the delivery and service system. If there was a conflict, this conflict was resolved by a general manager who understood both sides. Over time, the teams came together so that both the sales and fulfillment functions began to understand with great clarity the balance needed between revenue production and cost control.

BELL SPORTS SETS UP SEPARATE COMPANIES

Bell Sports, the maker of bicycle helmets, accessories, and other sporting goods, separated its customer-centric functions into a marketing company that purchases from several Bell-owned manufacturing companies. Here again, the marketing company focuses on the outside customer while the manufacturer simply serves the marketing company.

This is the ultimate customer-centric or Single Egg Organization. Each company, starting with the marketing company, must grow and make a profit. The marketing company is not distracted with manufacturing problems, which require a totally different discipline. The manufacturing companies are not distracted by growth problems, but understand that they must produce quality and cost to maintain their profitability. The marketing company was even given the freedom to purchase from outside vendors if the company-owned manufacturers didn't meet the customer requirements.

Each of these companies recognized the need to focus its people on the customer and also realized that the traditional structure generally produced internally oriented pillar suboptimization. By switching to the customer-centric organization and applying the system principles described in Part I, they were able to better focus on customer needs in a changing marketplace.

Consider your organization's structure. To what extent does it focus people on sustained, profitable growth?

The next chapter provides a very exciting and productive way to jumpstart your organization to become more customer focused. It is a concept used by Federal Express, Paddi Lund (the dental business), and many other companies that found their focus turned inward and had a desire to refocus employees quickly, simply, and without much cost.

THE HIERARCHY OF HORRORS

At Federal Express, as in most companies, the company believed that it had reached a balance between customer service and cost. It was called the 95% rule.

A curve demonstrated that to improve on-time delivery beyond 95% was not economically valid and that to do so would increase the price of the service beyond what was acceptable to the customer. Conversely, to drop below 95% would cost customers. Therefore, 95% was considered the optimum service level.

This is also true of warehousing and inventory. To have an item available beyond a certain percent of the time would mean overstocking and is therefore not economically viable. Again, in the warehousing example, the cost of stocking products that move very slowly would not justify having all products available 100% of the time.

Fred Smith has a way of standing back from the business and challenging the basic tenets of the business. One day he challenged the "95% rule"—a sacred cow since the very early days.

"If we handle a million packages a day and we mess up 5%, that means we mess up 50,000 packages a day," he reasoned. "And since one person ships to another, that means we've disappointed 100,000 people each day. It doesn't take a rocket scientist to figure out that before long you've disappointed everyone in America who ships or receives packages."

Then he created what he called a Hierarchy of Horrors. Of the 5% disappointments, what is the worst thing you can do to the customer? What is the next worst thing and so on? He and his senior management team identified eight major horrors.

For example, losing or damaging a package is the worst thing you can do. Delivering a package a couple of minutes late (right-day late) is the least-worst thing you can do and so on.

Then, to develop the feedback and relevance systems to focus employees on resolving these issues, they assigned relative values to each of the horrors.

For every lost or damaged package, they assigned 10 points. For every right-day late, they assigned one point. Then, under their feedback systems, they set up a method for measuring the number of incidences for each of the horrors they identified. The number of incidences times the points added up for a day was called the Service Quality Index.

The SQI is like the Dow Jones average. It provides one measurement that sums up how well the company delivers on its promise.

Fred's goal was to grow the company while lowering the SQI, and he and his management team set very specific goals and relevance factors around the SQI (SQI).

In the beginning, the SQI totaled more than 150,000 points per day, and specific average points per day goals were set. One-third of the managers' performance bonus was based on each manager's specific SQI goals. The SQI system also affected every manager in the company because every department had some part in meeting the SQI goals, either by reducing the frequency or resolving the problem to the customer's satisfaction.

The overall SQI system performance meant that every employee had to significantly improve his or her service quality. The index was well over 150,000 points per day, and, over time, the points have come down as the company's volume grew from 1 million packages per day to over 5 million packages per day.

Federal Express's on-time delivery percentage went from 95% to 99.7% (plus or minus) without adding significant costs to the operation. What made this possible is the total engagement of employees every step of the way.

One additional problem with this type of service measurement is that it measures what you give, not necessarily what the customer gets.

For example, the package arrives on time and in good condition, but the delivery courier is surly or discourteous. Therefore, one of the horrors could only be measured with customer perception, so Federal Express set up a system where it would call 1% of its customers every day and conduct a service-perception survey.

In effect, every employee's job was somehow related to the SQI. If you were a manager of pilots, you were measured on the pilot's ability to get the plane there on time and safely. This might involve identifying potential mechanical failures, flight delays, and other obstacles that the pilot could overcome to meet scheduled delivery times.

The system was now set up:

- Goals were set for the SQI.
- Goals were made relevant by tying them to the bonus structure.
- Feedback was set up using the SQI as the bottom-line service indicator.

Now for the actions...

Instead of senior management or even middle management taking actions to improve the SQI, the company involved its employees in small workgroups to tackle each of the issues. Hundreds and later thousands of people participated, and people found solutions and acted on them.

For example, the claims team tackled the problem of lost or damaged packages.

Certainly, others tackled this issue to attempt to get at the cause and to reduce the number of loss or damage incidences. The hub people looked for places where packages were damaged by equipment or lost in the massive Memphis hub operation.

Field people identified ways they could cut loss or damage and so on, but the claims team tackled it from a different perspective. This employee team from the claims department reasoned that, no matter how well you did, when you handle millions of packages each day to and from points around the world, you will lose or damage some. Therefore, the problem became one of taking care of the customers when they do have a problem, reducing the anger caused by the mistake, and capturing customers for life.

Management reasoned properly that the people to solve this problem were not managers, but the people who dealt with upset customers every day. Managers were not in a position to relate to the irate customer who just had an assembly line go down because the part was damaged or who had just lost a major contract because a document was lost. This relationship was very important to the commitment to solve the problem in a systemic way.

It is interesting that the people who answer the phone or deal in other ways directly with the customer in most companies are the people most qualified both to define and resolve customer needs that they experience through direct contact with the customer.

These frontline people know, even more than customers, what the horrors and needs are.

That may sound counterintuitive, but think about it.

You're a Federal Express customer and have used the company for years without incident. If someone asked you how important a loss or damage system was, you'd say "not very. They never screw it up." On the other hand, if you handled 50 irate customers a day and someone asked you that question, you'd respond with an entirely different answer, and you'd respond passionately.

Therefore, the claims people took it on. After working the problem for several weeks, they had a solution. "Give us a checkbook. We want to cut a check and mail it that day. We have the systems in place to know that we damaged or lost it. Why quibble and do what UPS does and delay it for 60 days? Give us the authority to cut a claims check that day and mail it."

After great debate, management agreed, and customers were pleasantly surprised with a fast resolution to their loss or damage problems. Customers who had a lost or damaged package were called for the perception interview. Their passion rating went through the roof.

It is interesting that customers will tolerate people making mistakes. What they will not tolerate is doing nothing about it. The people in the Federal Express claims department knew this.

Project teams were set up throughout the company to tackle one horror after another. They took actions to fix the problem first. If they couldn't fix it, they put in processes to at least give the customer more power over the mistake.

Now, that said, instantly resolving customer issues can cause other problems over time. Although most customers are relatively honest and will not take advantage, some will. As a result, Federal Express put in a tracking system to identify customers that have a high frequency of loss or damage. At a certain point of high loss or damage, the customer is questioned and a joint solution is developed.

For example, if there is high damage, the packaging is reviewed with the customer. If loss is high, the addresses are reviewed and so on.

Another example...

About the same time Federal Express was developing and implementing what Fred Smith called "The Hierarchy of Horrors," Paddi Lund, the dental office in Brisbane, Australia, was essentially doing the same thing (see Chapter 15), except he was doing it for a dental office, and he didn't call it the Hierarchy of Horrors.

Paddi and his staff identified all the reasons people hated going to a dentist. Things like pain, waiting, cost, smell, and so forth. They identified 37 reasons why people were unhappy going to a dental office. After they identified them, they ranked them to create the hierarchy.

Then, team members spent an hour each week in a meeting tackling each problem. Also, they began thinking about how to solve the horrors during their daily routine.

For pain, they developed the pain button. Paddi realized that 95% of what a dentist does in your mouth does not create pain. What creates pain is a stressed out dentist that is in a hurry and gets careless. All this is well and good, but try telling a patient that fact. You sit them down and tell them to trust you to not cause pain, and they obviously don't trust you.

Therefore, Paddi's team created a pain button. Patients hear the explanation and then are given a pain button. If they feel any pain, they simply press the button, and Paddi is alerted and stops what he is doing.

Paddi says that when he first implemented the pain button, he would get within 18 inches of the patient's mouth, and the pain button would go off. People were that nervous, but, after a couple of minutes, they would drop the pain button and were completely relaxed. I spoke to several patients who said the same thing. "After 30 seconds, I realized I really didn't need the pain button."

Waiting was handled by giving people their personal office with their name on the door. Additionally, you don't walk into a waiting room when you first arrive at the practice. You walk into a living room with a $5,000 espresso machine, Royal Doulton china, high-quality artwork, and so forth. You are not reminded of a dental office the minute that you walk in. You are reminded of a very pleasant and hospitable home. The doors are locked to create an experience like visiting a friend where you would knock on the door and be personally greeted.

Chapter 15 tells this story in more detail, but the Hierarchy of Horrors process was the same for the multibillion dollar Federal Express as it was for an eight-person dental office in Australia.

We have also used the Hierarchy of Horrors process in departments of large companies that were dealing only with internal customers, an auto dealership, and many other large and small organizations. We used it in the hospital discussed in Chapter 8.

The process is relatively simple.

There are two ways to go about it, which are best illustrated in the Federal Express and Paddi Lund examples.

One way is to identify the horrors at the top of the organization and then get teams of people to resolve the issues. The other way is to have your people identify the issues and then tackle them one at a time. The two also work well together. For example, when Fred Smith identified lost or damaged packages as a major horror, the claims team got together and identified the horrors within the horror so to speak.

A lost package is a greater horror than a damaged one. At least with a damaged package, I know what my options are. If a package is lost, it might be found later and so on. The team members were also able to identify the degree of horror by the customer's attitude on the phone and to develop ways of dealing with those degrees.

The basic approach to getting the employees involved is to bring 8 to 10 people together with a facilitator. The facilitator should not be anyone with a stake in the outcome of the group because this person will make judgments that dampen the group's passion to resolve the issue creatively.

The facilitator explains the process and simply lists the horrors on a flip chart. This sounds simple, and it is. However, good facilitators will draw people out by putting them in the clients' mind. They will say things like "see yourself coming into our office. What are you feeling? What is bothering you? What are you thinking?"

After the list is complete, the facilitator has each person get up and pick his or her top three or four horrors based on what that person believes would have the most impact on the customers' loyalty. You simply give each person a marker and let them place checks next to the horrors they believe are the worst. This creates the hierarchy.

Then management develops a task headline and guidelines for each and gives these tasks as projects to various teams or team members. For example, in the hospital's case, the task was "Handle our average emergency patient in less than an hour without increasing the cost." This would respond to the horror that was the waiting time.

While this is going on, you develop the measurement system (feedback) and the goals using the measurements (goals) and make solving these horrors relevant to the people who have the tasks (relevance).

Paddi Lund implemented a weekly profit-sharing system that made the horrors relevant to his office people. More important, he implemented a daily feedback system that made resolving the horrors very relevant to staff and patients every minute of every day.

Each of the tasks or horrors will go through an evolutionary process where the team will come up with ideas, take actions, see the results, and then go through the next iteration. Chapter 15 describes the dental team's evolution of eliminating smell as a horror in their office.

The Hierarchy of Horrors system is probably the easiest, most cost-effective, and best way to get·employees focused on their customers whether those customers are inside or outside the organization.

The Hierarchy of Horrors process helps people stand back from their daily routine long enough to put themselves in their customers' shoes and to view their service from their customers' perspective. After doing that, they become more sensitive to any customer problem, whether it fits in the horror system or not.

The Hierarchy of Horrors, like all change processes, depends on building a CustomerCulture where people adapt to and, in fact, embrace change as an exciting part of their job environment. The next chapter describes a change process that works for getting people excited about their role in building the CustomerCulture.

THE SEVEN DYNAMICS OF CHANGE

In the end, this book is about change, constant and never-ending change, and building an organization where change is second nature to all involved.

An organization that gives its people power over their own destiny, especially in the face of constant change and growth, is an organization with highly charged and energized people.

The core principle: People don't mind change. They mind being changed.

In order to understand that statement, it is necessary to understand more specifically why people resist being changed or even change itself. This chapter will describe the dynamics of change and will propose a process for dealing with change from a leader's perspective.

The change process described has been used to lay off people; implement new technologies; reorganize a company; and, in several other areas, get people seeing change as an opportunity for growth and advancement rather than something to be resisted.

The chapter starts with an exercise in change that you can use with your managers and employees to get them to understand experientially why they may want to resist change. After that experiential understanding, I review a process that deals with the dynamics and then provide examples of how the process has been used successfully.

DYNAMICS OF CHANGE EXERCISE

I attended a seminar in Australia where the facilitator conducted an exercise that drove home the dynamics of change. If you have a group of people and want them to begin to understand change and its dynamics, this is an interesting, fun, and productive exercise.

The exercise enables people to experience change in a fun way and drives home the point of why change is resisted and what to do about it.

Here is the exercise that can be conducted with small to infinitely large groups:

1. Have people stand up and organize in pairs. Ask them to follow your instructions carefully and do exactly as you say.

2. Give them one minute to face one another and identify their partner's appearance. Tell them that, in a minute, their partner will change their appearance and their task will be to identify what their partner has changed. Ask them not to talk or laugh. They will learn how long a minute can be.

3. Next have them turn away from their partner and make five changes to their physical appearance. Tell them to make the changes obvious because they want their partner to identify them. Give them one minute.

4. Have them face each other and identify the changes their partner made. Give them about one and a half minutes. After the time limit, proceed even if they're not done.

5. Have them turn away and make 10 more changes to their appearance. This always gets an "ahhhhh." Give them one and a half minutes.

6. Finally, have them face each other, identify the changes, and, "when they're done, sit down."

The process above is the experiential part of the exercise.

While they're going through the experience, write the seven dynamics on a flip chart or have it on a PowerPoint™ presentation and present one dynamic at a time. If it is a flip chart, use a piece of tape to uncover just one dynamic at a time.

On the flip chart or PowerPoint slide, write the dynamics of change. During change, the following dynamics occur:

1. People will feel uncomfortable and ill at ease.

2. People will feel alone.

3. People will feel that they can handle only so much change at a time.

4. People will look at the negative first.

5. People will believe there are not enough resources.

6. People will be at different levels of readiness.

7. Without outside influence, people will revert back to where they started.

Next, ask the audience the following questions as you go through each of the dynamics:

1. "How many of you felt uncomfortable and ill at ease during the exercise?" You'll find most of the audience will respond affirmatively here. Show the dynamic and explain it.

2. "How many of you felt alone?" Here, not many people felt alone because they were in the midst of a group of people all going through the same experience. Point out that this exercise doesn't demonstrate this very real dynamic of change very well.

3. "What was your feeling when I asked you to 'make 10 more changes?'" Here you may remind them of their "ahhhh" reaction. Point out that people can handle only so much change at a time.

   There is a corollary here. Ask how many of them had more fun making the second 10 changes than the first 5. You will find many people did. Often, when people are truly challenged, they will leave their comfortable state, get quite creative in solving difficult problems, and have fun in the process.

   At this point, I tell the story of working with an insurance company where the company had given a team of people the task of reducing the set-up time from 45 to 30 days.

When the team got together, it set its own goal of 10 days because that is what it believed was necessary for its customers. The team ended up getting very creative and setting up a new company in five working days.

4. "How many of you took something off?" Most did. Point out that people naturally look at the negative first when going through change. Generally, people look at what they will lose or have to give up during change.

5. "How many of you felt that there was no way you could make the second 10 changes?" The "ahhhh" came from a feeling of limitation when, in reality, after they get into it, most people find there are many changes they can make in their appearance. However, the initial feeling is always that there are not enough resources.

   Chapter 12 discussed working with a team of doctors, nurses, and administrators from a hospital. Its task was to reduce the emergency department time for patients from more than three hours to less than an hour on the average. The team's first reaction was to add doctors, nurses, and administrators. After the team got creative, it solved the problem without one additional person.

6. "How many of you didn't want any part of this?" Here you'll have experienced some who participated at a very minimal level or perhaps even not at all. People are at different levels of readiness for change. Some people love it and jump right in. Others are more reserved.

   The real value of this dynamic is to use the power of both sides. Where there is resistance to a change situation, there is usually good reason beyond some people's natural aversion to being told what to do. The process that follows values the person who resists, but balances those attitudes with people who thrive on change.

7. "This last dynamic is the most important and powerful. Look at your partner. How many of your partners appear essentially the same as when we started the exercise? I didn't tell you to 'put yourself back together' before you sat down. I simply asked you to 'identify the changes and when you're done, sit down.'"

This dynamic is the most powerful and the dynamic most important for those leaders attempting to manage change. Without outside influence, nearly all people will revert back to what is comfortable, which is usually the state before the change. This is particularly true of organizational change.

HOW TO DEAL WITH THE DYNAMICS OF CHANGE

Let's assume you understand these dynamics and are building the constantly evolving organization proposed in this book. How do you manage change understanding these dynamics?

Fred Smith is a master of change. Every year, during the formative stages, he would reorganize and give people different jobs just to avoid complacency and to drive change as the key dynamic of the organization.

After leaving Federal Express, I thought back to Fred's technique, not only for managing change, but for driving innovation. In fact, this process that he used naturally was the process that led to the innovation that became Federal Express and explains where the name "Federal Express" came from.

Tom Peters had interviewed Fred and learned that Fred, while a sophomore at Yale University, had written a term paper on the business concept that was Federal Express. He got a "C" on the term paper. People's natural reaction, when hearing this, is that professors wouldn't know a good business concept when they hear one.

After several years of hearing this story, I asked Fred one day, "Is that story true?"

"If you mean, did I write a 'C' term paper that ended up being Federal Express—yes it is. If you mean, did I describe the company as it is today—not even close. It was a dumb idea."

Fred went on to explain what the idea was and how it evolved into the Federal Express we know today.

Fred was studying economics in the early 60s. The Federal Reserve system has 12 banks geographically distributed throughout the United States. When a check is cashed at any bank that is from any other bank, it will go through a Federal Reserve bank to be cleared and sent back to the originating Federal Reserve bank.

When the two banks involved are served by different Federal Reserve banks, the check moves between these major banks. This takes time, and, because of the time, there was a tremendous "float," or the amount of money tied up while checks were en route between Federal Reserve banks. Generally, it took a week to 10 days to clear interreserve bank checks.

Fred's objective in the term paper was to create a business to reduce the float to one day by clearing the checks overnight, and that's what he wrote the term paper on. He named the concept and the company "Federal Express" as a way to clear checks between Federal Reserve banks overnight.

They say there is never anything truly new—just old ideas applied to new needs.

Fred's concept was to move checks between Federal Reserve banks the way that mail was originally sorted in rural areas. A train would go through a town and pick up a bag of mail for all other towns. En route to the next town, mail handlers, on the train, sorted the mail. When reaching the next town, they would drop off the bag for that town and pick up a bag for all other towns. As the train or trains completed a circular route, all mail eventually got sorted, and quite efficiently.

Fred's idea was to use two DC3s (the old internal combustion tail draggers produced in the early 30s and still in use today). He would start in Chicago with two planes. One plane would go toward the east, stopping in New York, Boston, Atlanta, Miami, and so forth, and one would go west to San Francisco, Seattle, Los Angeles, and so forth.

The concept was for each plane to land, pick up the checks for all other reserve banks, and sort and clear en route to the next city. That's the concept that Fred wrote the term paper on and got the "C."

When hearing this story, I asked Fred what his vision was at that time.

"Vision, smision. I just wanted to fly airplanes, but I wanted to make money at it and that ruled out carrying passengers."

I believe he meant that literally. He wanted to personally fly airplanes at that point. He had no idea of founding a $20 billion company.

After Yale, Fred went to Vietnam. Upon his return at age 27, he wanted to pursue his Federal Express idea.

This is where his process and the process of innovation came into play. He had a dumb idea, which at that point still seemed like a good idea to him, and he wanted to pursue it. While in Vietnam, as a Marine pilot, he had lined up some friends who could join with him to pilot the two DC3s. He also had a trust fund that would enable him to finance this new venture.

They say that all great new business innovations come from people outside the industry because they are not locked into existing paradigms. What they don't say is that most true innovation comes from dumb ideas that evolve into breakthrough business concepts.

Fred's process was generally to take an idea, study it in his mind until reasonably comfortable, and then present it to others for feedback. He would then work with others to develop the idea further. He would continue to do this until the idea became a concept that he was ready to act on.

The most important ingredient in Fred's process is that, as more and more people became involved, an excitement would develop not only in Fred, but in everyone else involved. In addition, as I mentioned earlier, in my opinion, commitment and excitement are 80% of what makes a new concept work. Fred's process not only improved the concept, but got people committed at the same time.

After Vietnam, Fred used the process to build the Federal Express term paper concept into the Federal Express that we experience today.

He started by putting the numbers to his idea and found that he needed more than 300 people to sort and clear the checks on the airplane between cities. Obviously, a DC3 wouldn't handle that load, so that didn't work.

New ideas are like newborn babies. They come out rather ugly and messy, but, with nurturing and support, they become functional and beautiful.

Most people, however, when developing an idea, give up when they discover their treasured dream of an idea won't work as they initially thought. Fred, however, doesn't work that way. He simply gets back in touch with what he is trying to accomplish and solves the problem at hand.

Because he couldn't sort and clear checks with people, he reasoned, "I'll find a machine to do it—one person feeding checks in and one taking them out and sorting them into 12 bags." He found a machine that would do it. It weighed more than a Boeing 747 so that wouldn't work, but he didn't give up.

He then realized that he had to sort and clear the checks on the ground. Because he lived in Little Rock, Arkansas, that was a logical place. He would pick up at each bank, fly to Little Rock, clear the checks on the ground, and fly the checks back to each city after the sort.

Because he still wanted to clear the checks overnight and because Boston, Seattle, Miami, and so forth were too far away to reach at DC3 speeds on an overnight basis, he would have to use jet aircraft. He reasoned he could only be four hours from the hub in order to provide overnight service.

Then he looked at the numbers again, but this time with the cost of jet aircraft in the equation. If he were able to get 50% of the checks moving between banks, it would cost more than $30 per check for the overnight system. Unless I had a very large amount in a specific check, I couldn't afford $30 to reduce the float a week, so that didn't work.

Fred stood back and looked at his system. He had discovered a way to move things overnight between all points in the United States. The next question was "Is there a need?" He commissioned two market research studies that both drew the same conclusion. There was a need for reliable overnight service between all points in the United States.

This is the point where Fred was ready to take major risks and start the company. The rest is history.

What has all this to do with the dynamics of change?

Fred's process is to look constantly for better ways of doing things, which means change for everyone around him. He has a process that, in effect, understands the seven dynamics of change. It is a process that understands systems and change in a way that evolves ideas to actionable solutions and, most important, gets and keeps extraordinary commitment to the solution.

THE TWO INGREDIENTS TO INNOVATIVE SUCCESS

My experience tells me that two ingredients are necessary for effective innovation.

First is a better solution. This might mean technology or simply a better way to move packages. It is a better way to accomplish something.

Second is the commitment to the solution. Anything new throws up enormous obstacles that must and can be overcome to the extent that the people involved are committed to finding the solution. If they are not committed, however, the company and the concept go under with the enormous obstacles that any new business faces during its birth.

Of the two ingredients (concept and commitment), I believe commitment is 80% of the stew. As the innovation that became Federal Express demonstrated, the original idea evolved into a life-changing business innovation only because Fred was committed to "fly airplanes," not to fly airplanes to clear checks overnight.

Fred's process not only evolves effective solutions, but it also gains enormous commitment from the people involved because it understands the dynamics of change.

WHAT IS THE PROCESS AND HOW IS IT COMPATIBLE WITH SYSTEMS THINKING?

Fred had a vision to fly airplanes without carrying passengers. His values began with the need to get people solidly behind whatever he was trying to do.

Now let's look at his specific process. It is quite simple and if followed to the letter, nearly always advances an idea toward a solution while engaging people's commitment to the idea. The process can be used within a person's head when first considering an idea, or it can be used with trusted associates, family members, or large groups of people to initiate major change.

It goes as follows:

1. Present the idea. Most people want to button up the idea as a solution because they don't want their idea rejected. Fred would certainly work the idea in his head for a period, but then quickly express the idea to others. Those others might begin with more conceptually oriented people who could work with him, but also might include drivers, pilots, or anyone who might have some insight into the obstacles that might get in the way of the idea's success.

   Remember the overriding principle: People don't mind change. They mind being changed.

   By presenting change ideas before they become actions, people are given the opportunity to be part of the change rather than being changed. People feel far more comfortable (Dynamic 1) when they are part of the change. When done with groups of people, they also don't feel alone in the process (Dynamic 2).

2. Identify the pluses. One dynamic of change is that people look for what is wrong first. They see the negative first (Dynamic 4). It is very easy to "throw out the baby with the

bath water" at this stage of change development. It is important to focus on what is positive first to get and to keep the energy level high.

In the story of Federal Express, it would have been very easy to focus on the facts that the original idea wouldn't work. Fred kept his vision in mind and helped people focus on the pluses before he let them trash the idea. He would insist on "What do you like about this idea?" as he engaged people in the concept.

3. Have people express concerns or obstacles as "How to..." instead of "you can't put 300 people on an airplane." You might state the problem as "how to sort and clear checks overnight without 300 people on an airplane," or "that's too expensive" stated as "how to make it cost-effective."

   This is important. People will often state an obstacle as unsurmountable. This does two things. First, it generates a defensive response from the people with the ideas. They're forced into defending their ideas rather than jointly looking for solutions. It doesn't engage the two or more people into finding solutions.

   Dynamic 3 is that people can handle only so much change at a time. This process engages people in getting creative about the change and helps reduce this obstacle to change.

   This step also deals with those people who resist all change by giving them the opportunity to voice their concerns. More often than not, there is an element of truth to the resistance caused by people being at different levels of readiness for change.

4. Work the problems together by getting ideas on how to resolve the issues. Here is where people get involved in solving the problems together. Ideas flow to resolve the concerns. Some hit and some don't. It doesn't matter.

This process starts with attempting to resolve the show-stopper concerns (getting 300 people or a heavy machine on an airplane to sort and clear checks overnight)."

Here again, this collaborative process makes people part of the change, so it therefore does not put people in the situation of being changed. At the end of this chapter, I will discuss how this process was applied to a layoff where people felt powerless in the process of a company cutting back.

5. Develop next steps. People participating in evolving a solution believe that their work was worthwhile if action results. It is important to define what, who, and when for each of the actions that may result from the process.

6. Follow-up. The last dynamic of change and the most important one is that people will revert back to where they started without outside intervention. If the next step involved an action, it is important that someone follow up on the commitment. If the follow-up is not there, there will be little change with this process.

Some examples of the change process in action are now given.

Reducing the Workforce

This is an example of using the process to resolve an issue of commitment during a time where change shakes commitment.

Problem

A company with 50 employees had to lay off 25% of its workforce. It had explored other options, but it finally came down to a significant reduction of workforce.

USUAL METHOD

Top management determines who will go and issues an order to make it happen. People are being changed.

SOLUTION

Top management appointed a six-person team to meet for a day and to determine who should be laid off. They began the meeting by explaining the reason for the layoff and what it meant to the survival of the company and the people. (Present the idea and the goal.)

It was explained that other options had been reviewed and that this team's goal was to identify the 12 people who had to leave to ensure the continued survival of the enterprise and to save the remaining jobs.

The team met in a facilitated session, reviewed the goal, and began its work. Within six hours, team members had a plan to lay off the 12 people. They had identified the people or jobs they could best give up. More important, they each volunteered to take two people who were losing their jobs to breakfast or lunch, explain the process, and explain why those people lost their jobs.

One of the team members actually volunteered to leave the company. She realized that her job was no longer necessary and, given the struggle and the logic of the layoff process, solved the problem.

The net result was that 12 people left with caring and dignity. The company's service never skipped a beat, and morale remained high under the circumstances.

People don't mind change. They mind being changed.

THE HUDSON RIVER RUNWAY

This is an example of using the process to find a creative solution to a very difficult problem.

PROBLEM

For a while, Federal Express considered an idea of creating a business passenger airline in order to better use its high-cost airplanes. Fred's idea was an airline that served cities downtown-to-downtown. For example, Chicago would be served from Megs Field (close to downtown), Dallas by Love Field, and so forth, rather than O'Hare and Dallas Fort Worth.

New York was the problem. Newark, LaGuardia, and Kennedy are all more than an hour from downtown during high-traffic periods when most business people want to travel.

SITUATION

I was in the process of building the superhub for Federal Express in Memphis. Our general contractor was the Austin Company, the builders of the largest building in existence at that time, Boeing's 747 manufacturing plant. Fred and I were in New York and had been invited to have dinner with Austin's president.

SOLUTION

During dinner, Fred looked at Austin's president and said in a matter-of-fact tone, "Art, how could we build a runway in the Hudson River?" While Art was recovering, Fred went on to explain his downtown-to-downtown concept. Then he said, "I know it's ridiculous, but, if you could do it, what would be the pluses?"

Art, probably fighting every business paradigm he had learned over the years, decided to play the game. "Well, it would differentiate Austin from every other builder. It would show that, given the commitment, people can accomplish the impossible." He went on and, as he did, I noticed he began to get excited about the prospect even though his better sense told him it could not be done.

Then Fred asked what would get in the way. "How to find the billions that would be required to get the permits, buy the waterfront properties, pay off government officials, and so forth."

Fred went back to the original vision with one of his concerns: How to get within 10 minutes of downtown New York, preferably Wall Street.

I had grown up in New Jersey near Sandy Hook, which is just a few miles by water (Raritan Bay) from downtown New York. Therefore, I suggested we put a runway on Sandy Hook and use a helicopter to go across the bay. We all immediately realized that if you had a helicopter service, you could still use the existing airports.

Art, working with Boeing, reminded us that Boeing had an airboat that could travel across water at 80 miles an hour. As we developed the solution, we realized that, if Sandy Hook was available, we had a solution to a downtown airport.

As it turned out, Sandy Hook was possible, but Federal Express scrapped the idea of a business passenger airline.

I use these examples only as a way to show how the change system works to find better solutions and commitment to those solutions.

CustomerCulture is about change and about evolutionary and revolutionary systems for managing change. Good solutions come from the combination of a better solution and people's commitment to that solution. The process shown in this chapter, when followed methodically, produces both for the innovative spirit in leaders.

This chapter ends the second part of the book, reflecting the application of building a CustomerCulture where every employee is focused on increasing value to the customers, fellow employees, and owners.

The next part ties it all together with the Paddi Lund story of an outrageous small business that is totally customer centered and very successful (see Chapter 15). Finally, I would be remiss if I didn't apply the principles in my current new venture. As a result, Chapter 16, "Anatomy of a Start-Up," demonstrates in fast-frame speed how CustomerCulture speeds innovation where it is most naturally applied—in a start-up situation. Finally, Chapter 17 outlines how CustomerCulture is built in turnaround situations.

THE RESULTS

The first part covered the theory about building a strong culture and the power of culture to influence and, in fact, direct people to focus on and serve their customers at higher and higher levels.

The second part provided more specific applications of the theory in practice, which enables companies to take specific actions to use the theory to build a more customer-focused organization.

This third part shows how a CustomerCulture is built in a small dental business, a technology start-up, and as part of a turnaround process.

Whether internal or external to an organization, we all have customers. If we apply the dental office principles, and indeed the principles proposed in this book, to small groups that then become part of progressively larger and larger organizations, countries, and so forth, we build a better world—one where all people focus on delivering more value to those they come into contact with.

15

THE PADDI LUND STORY

" Take your name out of the phone book, stop all advertising, lock your doors, and fire 75% of your customers."

This is the advice of Paddi Lund, who runs an eight-person dental office in Brisbane, Australia. If there is an ideal business, this is it: very profitable, zero turnover, happy employees and owner, and an integrated home and business life for all employees.

More important, this is a story of business transformation from average to extraordinary over a period of a decade.

The story started about 12 years ago. Paddi was very unhappy, working 60 hours a week and making average dental pay.

He was stressed out and at the end of his rope. So much so, he seriously considered suicide. He investigated various ways to take his life from slashing his wrists in a bathtub of warm water to leaping off a bridge in Brisbane. He learned that wrist slashing took too long and bridge leaping might end up with one being dragged from the mud and still alive.

Then he asked a critical question—a question that we all need to ask frequently.

"If the goal of life is happiness, however one defines it, why would I spend the prime years of my life and the prime hours of those years at a job that makes me unhappy?"

He began to explore why he was so unhappy and learned that dentists commit suicide 100 times more than the average person. On the verge of taking his own life, he was open and ready to hear the answers to why his dental practice made him unhappy.

He started by asking his employees, who told him honestly that his dental practice was a terrible place to work. "People, first and foremost Paddi, were rude to each other." His employees couldn't wait to leave each day and were happy only on Friday afternoon when they foresaw the state they called POETS (Piss

Off Everything, Tomorrow's Saturday)—the Australian version of TGIF (Thank God It's Friday).

After listening to his employees and deciding not to take his life, Paddi created a vision that he describes as dental happiness— an oxymoron to most people. He became obsessed with developing a happiness-centered business where people (customers, employees, and owners) truly enjoyed being.

Going through the CustomerCulture process, here is what Paddi did:

1. Paddi developed the vision of a happiness-centered business where people loved to work and clients (new name for patients) loved to visit and do business.

2. Values were set in the form of the Courtesy System. The team came up with rules of conduct that were generally acceptable to everyone working there. This was perhaps the most important phase because it defined the culture that set the boundaries for everything that followed.

3. Goals were established covering service, happiness, and revenue. These goals balanced the needs of customers, employees, and the owner.

4. Goals were made relevant with a weekly profit-sharing system and by daily discussions about happiness and the vision that all could relate to.

5. A daily feedback system was put in place in a 10-minute daily meeting where people would rate their happiness on a scale of 1 to 10, their service on the same scale, and the actual revenues produced. One employee called the happiness indicator the "stressometer" because it showed that stress and happiness were inversely proportional.

6. After this system was in place, the people began to meet weekly to identify the obstacles and to develop actions to resolve them.

They started their action phase by defining their "Hierarchy of Horrors" (see Chapter 13) and beginning to understand why they were unhappy. They quickly decided they were unhappy because they were around people most of the time who didn't want to be there—people that didn't want to be around them.

This phenomenon describes why dentists commit suicide more than the average person. We hunger, Paddi reasoned, for human companionship, and when we're around people who don't want to be around us, for whatever reason, we get depressed.

Therefore, in order to create dental happiness, they had to create an environment where people wanted to be. They decided that they had to start with the reasons people didn't want to be there.

For example, people don't like pain. They don't like spending time and money with few perceived results and so on.

In summary, going to the dentist is a negative experience.

They defined 37 different horrors to start with, which included things like pain, smell, waiting, value, time spent, and so forth.

Then, they (all employees) began by taking one at a time and coming up with ideas and actions that would resolve the issue.

They started with smell. Smell is an interesting phenomenon. It is one of the more powerful unconscious motivators of human behavior. If you smell something that reminds you of a bad childhood experience, you will move into a negative mood, and the cause will be unconscious. Also, if you smell something that reminds you of a positive experience, you will move into a positive mood.

The smell of a dental office generally moves people to a negative mood. I know in my case, I am reminded of the childhood experience before Novocaine and high-speed drills. I didn't like being there.

Also, on the positive side, people attempting to sell their homes have proven that a smell of fresh-baked bread in a home for sale increases the likelihood of purchase.

Paddi's team took it on. It sounds simple. Come up with a smell that will emit positive emotions. They started by putting perfume in the air conditioning system. As part of their feedback, they would constantly ask if people noticed anything different. When they asked about the smell, they got feedback. "It smells like a house of ill repute," came the answer, or, as my friend says, "a house of negotiable affections."

Well, depending on the client's experience, that didn't elicit the experience they were trying to create.

Then, they decided to make coffee. Coffee has a smell that generally reminds people of a pleasant experience. The problem is that it goes away quickly, so they decided to grind coffee throughout the day and give some of it to their clients. This cost too much. They were grinding 10 pounds a day.

Then, one of the care nurses (their name for the support staff) came up with the idea of buying an oven and baking "dental biscuits." This idea hit big with the clients. Not only did they arrive to a great smell, but they received a gift of the biscuits at the end of the visit. The biscuits were a special recipe formulated by one of the care nurses to make sure there were no negative dental effects.

As Paddi said later, "It was fun seeing grown men walking across the parking lot with their little basket of dental biscuits."

Many of their clients have asked for the recipe for their dental biscuits.

Pain was an interesting challenge. Paddi explains that pain is a function of what the dentist is doing in your mouth and that 95% of what dentists do is not painful. After all, he will tell you, they are drilling to remove decay, not nerves.

That's easy for him to say. He's not the one who's in the chair.

This is people's natural reaction when told that something painful doesn't really need to be painful. After all is said and done, when it comes to the customer experience, perception is reality, and my perception, as the perception of most of Paddi's clients, is that having a drill in your mouth is painful. I don't care what you say to me.

Well, the success structure provided that feedback as well, so the team developed what is known as the pain button, which was a simple device that clients hold in their hand that would tell the dental staff that the client was experiencing pain. It was hooked up to a simple buzzer that would alert the dentist. Then, the dentists (Paddi and one other) would rethink their work to make sure it was not painful.

When the dentists began the use of the pain button, Paddi described how it worked in the client's personal room and handed the pain button to the client after he or she was comfortably settled in the dental chair. He said it was interesting in the beginning. He would get within 18 inches of the client's mouth, and the pain button was pushed—talk about perception being reality.

I spoke with several patients, and they all said the same thing. None of them believed him, but, after 30 seconds of drilling, all, to a person, relaxed and dropped the pain button—although nearly all said they kept it close. They had eliminated pain from the reasons people don't like going to a dental office.

One by one, the team took on the horrors, and, one by one, it eliminated them.

The perception of waiting was cured by not having waiting rooms and by never being late. In fact, if the staff were more than a minute late getting to the clients, they would give the clients an $80 bottle of champagne for their trouble. Because they shared the profits, this created incredible relevance for running the practice on time.

Such relevance eventually led to the firing of the vast majority of clients. The reason most practices are late is that a patient shows up late and, to fit him or her in, the practice begins shuffling the schedule. Soon everything and everyone is late.

In this case, the team identified the types of clients it wanted to do business with. What's more, it identified the types of clients that would add to the dental happiness vision. Clients that were perpetually late were not clients it wanted, so it gradually weeded them out.

If someone came in late, the client's care nurse would sit down with the client, explain how important it was to run on time, and suggest he or she reschedule the time to another day or week. If that didn't work for the client, the care nurse suggested that the practice should refer the client to another dentist.

Over time, this type of honest treatment and adherence to the vision, goals, and values led to a turnover of 75% of the clients. The team used a set of guidelines to identify each client as A, B, C, or D and developed a plan to move the D and C clients to other dentists and to move the B clients either to As or out the door.

A clients are people who want to practice preventive dentistry, want their mouth to be healthy, and respect their health in general. Most important, A clients enjoy life and respond to people who care. In short, they are people who want to be happy. Several indicators of these people became apparent. They show up on time, they pay their bills, and they take care of their teeth and generally want the best in treatment.

"Different strokes for different folks," as Paddi explains it. He tells the story of a client that did not fit the A or B profile. This client worked in a meat-processing plant, smoked, and clearly was not concerned about his dental health. One day, he came in with a severe toothache and, because of long-term dental problems, told Paddi he wanted dentures.

Paddi wanted clients who wanted to keep their teeth, so now was a good time to refer this client to another dentist. He explained that he didn't believe in dentures, but that he understood the client's desires and would be quite happy to refer the client to a dentist that could better serve his needs.

Paddi remembers going to a bar and seeing the dentist to whom he referred the client. He didn't want to face the dentist, but was finally spotted by the other dentist and confronted. To Paddi's disbelief, the dentist was very happy for the referral and thanked him profusely. He said that he had taken good care of the client, given him dentures, and was paid promptly.

Paddi was somewhat dismayed to realize that the client wanted exactly what the other dentist had and was pleased enough to pay promptly, which was something he never did with Paddi's practice.

After that experience, he realized that you can't be all things to all people. You pick your customer base and do all you can to attract the type of people you want to serve and who want the service you offer. In doing that, you reject a good number of potential customers. "Your message," he points out, "is best when it is very seductive to some, but turns away the majority." This is a very important point that few marketers understand. Many marketers want to communicate everything they are and, as a result, don't deliver a compelling message to the people who really want what they have.

Over time, the team developed a by-referral-only practice by asking each A client to refer someone like himself or herself to the practice. Gradually, it sent the Cs and Ds to other practices by either referring them out or having them leave because they were not satisfied with what the practice was becoming.

In the last few years, the practice has become by-invitation-only, meaning that you cannot go to the practice without first being invited.

Here is the bottom line.

Twelve years ago, Paddi was making average dental pay working 60 hours a week, had high turnover, was stressed out, and was depressed.

Today, Paddi makes 3.5 times the average dental pay, works 23 hours a week, has zero employee turnover, and is the happiest human being I know.

Paddi and his team were clear about one thing. Growth meant only growing toward happiness, not growing in size. Paddi is a minimalist and doesn't know how much money he has in the bank. He was crystal clear about his goal of happiness was at the cost of becoming big or building a multioffice practice. He wanted happiness. If money came, which it did, that was fine, but not necessary beyond a minimal amount.

My first visit to the Patrick Lund Dental Practice was quite interesting. I had seen Paddi speak at a seminar in Brisbane. I had heard many business leaders get up and describe successes similar to what I heard from Paddi, so I was quite skeptical. However, I had my way of checking it out—interviewing customers and employees.

I went to Paddi after his talk and asked him if he would mind if I visited his practice and spoke with several of his employees and customers. He was getting ready for a six-week trip to Europe and said that it was fine for me to visit as long as I gave him feedback after my interviews. I agreed. It was interesting that he could leave for six weeks and his practice wouldn't skip a beat.

The next week I received a hand-drawn color map telling me how to get to the practice. This was necessary because there is no sign, only a golden apple indicating the practice. I drove up, parked, and went to the door. The door was locked. I rang the doorbell.

About 20 seconds later, Marilyn came to the door and said, "Hi Mike, I'm Marilyn." She did not say, "Hi Michael" or "Hi Mr. Basch," but "Hi Mike." That simple greeting said so much. When my friend Paul called to make the appointment, the receptionist went through a simple list of questions, one of which was "How does he like to be called or referred to?"

"Why the doorbell and locked doors?" I asked.

"We want your experience to be like a home. When friends come to your home, they ring the bell, and you greet them—sometimes with a hug, sometimes with a handshake, but always in a friendly, caring manner. We want to duplicate that."

Marilyn led me to a door that said "Welcome Mike Basch." We went in and sat down. The room wasn't very large. I noticed that Marilyn left the door open a crack.

"Why leave the door open?" I asked.

"This is your room, but it is small. We've found, over the years, that to close the door is claustrophobic and to leave it open violates your privacy, so we leave it open a crack."

We sat down and began the interview. Pretty soon, there was a knock at the door. "Hi Mike, I'm Joanne. Paul said you enjoy blueberry muffins with decaffeinated cappuccino. Is that correct?" As I said yes, she came in with a silver tray with Royal Doulton china on it

This was blowing me away. Every other place, if you got coffee, it was in a plastic cup, and you served yourself, and again, I observed the use of my name and finding out what kinds of things I enjoyed eating and drinking.

These are just a few examples of hundreds of details that demonstrate both caring and quality. Earlier in this book, I mentioned UPS's obsession with clean trucks and its reasoning that it conveys a sense of quality.

The same is true for a dental office. For the most part, people have no sense of quality dental work as long as it feels right when the work is done, so quality must be communicated in other ways—quality tea service, clean restrooms, quality environment, and so forth.

As Joanne served us, Marilyn mentioned that they celebrate tea service in silence in honor of the server rather than continuing to talk and ignore her presence.

I was beginning to experience an interesting phenomenon. People will generally adapt to their environment very quickly. If you have clear and certain rules, the people entering the practice will follow those rules generally without question.

An example is on-time dental service delivery. If the practice is always on time and you never have to wait and, if you are late, they will not slot you in, you will begin to show up on time.

After some discussion and my realization of the reality of what I was experiencing, I wanted to find out if this could be duplicated, so I asked:

"Marilyn, if your husband was transferred to Sydney and you went with him and went to work for a dentist there, could you create the same atmosphere and success you have here?"

She looked at me strangely. "You mean I leave here and go to Sydney with my husband? I'd divorce him before I'd leave this practice."

Obviously, this was tongue-in-cheek, but she made her point.

She went on to explain some of the milestones in the transition from average to extraordinary.

One milestone was a time when the care nurses would congregate around the receptionist counter. Paddi didn't like the counter because it presented a barrier to human relationship. "He would ask us not to congregate. We would agree, but as soon as he was out of sight, we'd congregate. One Saturday, he enlisted my husband and his chain saw. Paddi and my husband came in together and cut the counter up in several pieces and left them on the floor for us to congregate around on Monday."

Clearly, this made a statement about Paddi's commitment to dental happiness.

She talked about the "stressometer" and how staff members would meet each day to review the day and discuss their relative happiness. "It occurred in stages. At first, we all were an 8 or 9 on the scale (1 to 10 with 10 very happy). Then, we began to discuss what happiness really meant. Most of us dropped to a 2 or 3, and we began to open up about what made us unhappy. It was stress. Therefore, we developed the Courtesy System to reduce stress. We would rate our own happiness and then talk about what would make it a 10."

Joanne was 19 years old and had worked in the practice for about 5 months. I spoke with her and asked her about her goals. She replied, "I want to get married and have children. I want to study to become a dental hygienist. Most important, I want to be here for the rest of my career."

In the dental industry, employee turnover is more than 60%, so this was a very unusual goal. I asked why. She replied that she was loved here. She went on. "I grew up in a very loving family, but here it's even better." I asked her to tell me whether there was any specific example she could give me.

"Yes," she replied with a tear coming to her eye. "One day during our afternoon meeting, Pat said to me that she was unhappy that day because I had said something to her that made her upset. I really wanted to fit here, so I asked her what it was. She replied that she couldn't remember.

"I went home that night and didn't sleep well. I kept trying to remember what I had done. The next day I came in and went to my work station to find a large bouquet of flowers with a note from Pat basically apologizing for bringing an issue up when she couldn't provide the detail. I cried and went in and hugged Pat.

"I'll never forget that living of our Courtesy System value 'when someone is upset by your actions, apologize and make restitution.' At that point, I really got the Courtesy System, so I'll be here the rest of my life if it is possible."

During my visit, I spoke to several clients. One had traveled from Sydney at an expense of over $800 to come to the practice. He had written a note about being treated with more dignity, respect, and caring than five-star resorts.

Summarizing the experience, I left feeling relaxed and focused. I had just visited what I still consider today, eight years later, probably the most ideal business environment on the planet. It is financially successful and brings happiness to all who touch it.

What has this all got to do with a major corporation and why present the example here?

Paddi Lund's progress from depression to happiness and from mediocre to success as a business underlines the potential of any organization large or small to build cultures that truly focus on customers, employees, and owners.

Clearly, Paddi formulated the experience he was trying to create, his vision, and described it in one simple statement: dental happiness.

He worked with his team to define the Courtesy System that created the value system. This value system defined the guidelines and rules staff members followed when working with one another.

Paddi and his team set happiness and business goals realizing that a business cannot remain a happy place to be unless it is profitable as a business. He made sure the goals were balanced in the sense of serving the customer (referral index), the employee (happiness index), and the owner (revenue and profit).

He developed his relevance system with weekly profit sharing. Many companies align goals with a profit-sharing program where everyone wins, but lose relevance in the timing by making it quarterly or yearly. Very few people take actions today to earn something a year away. Paddi's weekly system keeps people focused on doing those things they need to do to meet or exceed their revenue goals. The weekly profit sharing is not a great deal of money, but it is a very meaningful scoreboard.

The daily meetings used feedback around happiness (employee and client) to develop a very deep sense of relevance and teamwork to resolve whatever issues that made the environment an unhappy place to be.

The full feedback system was quite simple. Revenue, happiness, and client referrals were reported and discussed daily and reported weekly. If the index was negative, a brief discussion would ensue, and time would be allocated at the weekly meetings to brainstorm ideas and take the appropriate actions to resolve the issue.

The Paddi Lund story illustrates the potential for building a strong CustomerCulture in any size business. When you boil it all down to the one necessary ingredient to Paddi's success, it was his incredible commitment to dental happiness.

As in most great stories, there is a postscript.

The natural congruity that comes from implementing such a culture as Paddi implemented spills over into personal life.

As one might expect, Paddi's personal life had taken a turn for the better as well. Well into the decade of transformation, his sister discovered she had cancer and asked Paddi to take care of one of her sons. The child had been diagnosed with Attention

Deficit Disorder (ADD). Evidently, he was incorrigible. He had no friends and barely got by in school, and no one wanted to be around him. Paddi agreed to take him in and do what he could.

The first thing Paddi did was sit the boy down and explain the rules.

"My goal in life is to be happy. I know that I am able to meet all of your needs and probably most of your wants, but I ask something in return. I insist that you follow the Courtesy System."

He went through the eight rules of courtesy behavior one at a time. "When you want something, say 'please.' When someone gives it to you, say 'thank you.' When someone thanks you, say 'you're welcome.'" He went through each rule in great detail, asking to make sure the boy understood each rule.

To get dinner, the boy had to ask for dinner with a "please." The boy was obviously in rebellion and decided not to follow any rules, particularly this rule. Therefore, he didn't eat for several days. As he discovered that his behavior wasn't going to get him any attention, or worse yet, something to eat, he decided to try at least that rule and asked for something to eat with a "please."

Gradually, over the ensuing months, he discovered that life could be pretty good if he developed the Courtesy discipline and followed all of the rules. His grades began to improve, and friends and relatives began to come around. It wasn't long after that his brother came to live with Paddi as well.

The last I heard, the family is fully functional, and both boys are at the top of their class with plenty of friends.

Paddi Lund's system works. It has worked in other dental offices, accounting offices, and all kinds of large and small businesses, but, like any other major culture change, it requires incredible commitment by the leader of the family or organization that desires to implement it.

Because the Courtesy System is the driving force behind Paddi's success, it is shown in greater depth here. The companies I have worked with that have implemented the Courtesy System have experienced dramatic increase in the quality of customer relationships and productivity.

THE COURTESY SYSTEM

The Courtesy System consists of eight rules or values that, when practiced consistently and with commitment to their underlying meaning, improve the quality of employee and customer relationships and productivity. These values, although very simple in nature, are very profound in their effect on workgroups. They essentially create a CustomerCulture, especially for smaller teams and workgroups.

1. **Greet and farewell.** When you come in to work in the morning, you go to whoever is there and greet them in a very specific way. You look them in the eye and greet them personally using their name and touching them in some way. It might be a hug, handshake, or just a touch on the shoulder. When you leave in the evening, you go through the same routine. The purpose of this rule is to get people relating to one another in a pleasant way at the beginning and ending of each day. This essentially sets the tone for the day.

2. **Speak very politely.** When you want something, you use the word "please." When someone gives you something, you say "thank you," then "you're welcome," and so on. It is amazing how people are generally very demanding and don't use the word "please." This sets up a very small dynamic that can escalate to anger and ill treatment of peers to each other. The purpose here is simple civility.

When people are polite with each other, it creates a more harmonious culture.

3. **Apologize and make restitution.** When someone feels wronged by your action, you apologize and take an action to back up the words. Joanne's story of how Pat bought her flowers and gave her a note when she couldn't tell her what the issue was is an example of this value. The purpose here is to identify relationship issues as they occur and then use more than words to heal the chasm between the two people. This rule is applied at the practice whether the wrong was intentional or not. The assumption is that if you feel hurt by my actions, it is up to you to express it and up to me to correct it.

4. **Use positive conversation.** When conversing, you use positive conversation. Even when dealing with issues, the approach is generally positive. Words such as "let's work out a solution" are used rather than "this doesn't work." This value gets people seeing the glass half full, not half empty. The purpose of this value is to get team members thinking and acting positively. This creates a positive, can-do attitude among team members.

5. **Talking about problems.** Talk about problems openly and honestly and as challenges to be overcome by the team. Don't fix the blame, but rather discuss the cause and what can be done to fix the problem. Another rule here is that if you have a problem with another person, you don't discuss it with others. The purpose of this value is to make sure problems are not ignored and are dealt with as a team or personal issue and never swept under the rug.

6. **Talking about people.** If you have a problem with someone or even positive things to say about someone and he or she is not present, you use his or her name in every sentence as if he or she is there and talk as if he or she is

present. Most workgroups have cliques and people often talk behind people's backs. This is a very destructive process. The purpose of this value is to confront issues between people directly and embrace every member of the group as a valued team member. If this cannot occur for whatever reason, it is best for the person to leave, as opposed to causing workgroup dysfunction.

7. **Blame a system.** Often, workgroups tend to blame people, not systems, for lack of performance. It has been proven that the work flow or cultural process or system is responsible for poor performance over 95% of the time, yet people often want to blame others rather than act on changing the system that drives performance. The purpose of this value is to get people looking consciously at how they work together rather than to place blame on people. Fix the problem, not the blame.

8. **Tell the truth.** Similar to Frank Chamberlain's approach discussed in Chapter 17, this value asks people to express the truth openly, responsibly, and honestly. For example, one time the dental practice did not send work in to the dental lab on time and when the client came to get the lab work completed on his mouth, the care nurse had to admit her mistake openly and honestly, even though it meant rescheduling for another day. The client was very forgiving and openly appreciated the honesty. Trust builds with honesty. The purpose of this value is to build trust among employees and clients.

To the extent these values can be inculcated into a workgroup, the results are magical. Turnover goes away, productivity goes up, customers and other visitors enjoy being there, and the work environment changes in very positive ways.

16

Anatomy of a Start-Up: Innovation in Action

Presently, I am involved in my 12th start-up and feel I would be remiss if I didn't describe the process and results of applying the principles proposed in this book in a start-up situation. Please keep in mind that this is a culture in formation with the ultimate outcome reasonably certain, but not yet experienced.

This story shows the power of implementing CustomerCulture principles during the period when the company's systems, habits, and sense of team are in their infant stages. This chapter demonstrates the power of innovation in action as an ongoing way of doing business.

The company, although nearly five years old, actively began selling about eight months prior to this writing. In that period of eight months, there is very little that has not changed as is the case in most start-ups.

Venture capital people generally look at the executive team as the primary driver for their decision to invest in a new venture. This is done for good reason. A solid executive team will do what is required to succeed, and, in any start-up, that means creatively embracing change every step of the way. More important, in my opinion, is that a solid executive team will pay attention to and implement a high-performing culture.

Nearly all start-ups begin by making lots of assumptions—assumptions that are eventually tested in the court of customer acceptance. A solid management team will constantly pay attention to the success or failure of these assumptions. The team members will also see the reality that these are assumptions, not based on fact, but on opinion, and must be measured carefully as the company grows.

My experience tells me that, in nearly all cases, the assumptions are sometimes close and sometimes not, but all times they must be revised as the feedback of customer acceptance or rejection comes in.

For example, during the Federal Express start-up, our assumption was that customers would be willing to use a pickup book to list their shipments similar to UPS's shipping paperwork system at the time. However, air shipments costing $20 were handled differently by customers than ground shipments costing $2. Companies wanted to track the department shipping by air and needed an audit trail for individual shipments. As a result, we had to quickly scrap the pickup book in favor of the more acceptable airbill system used by air-freight forwarders at the time. This is just one example of where the operational assumptions changed as a result of continual feedback from customers.

The CustomerCulture structure described in this book simply accelerates a very natural process taken by thinking business leaders—the process that starts with a hypothesis, goes to market with it, gets the reaction of potential customers, makes the change, and goes to market again and so on.

The start-ups I have personally been involved with all had a vision to change an industry or make a major change in cultural habits. There is very little known for certain in these kinds of start-ups. The best that can be hoped for is to take an action, listen carefully to the reaction, and then react to that input by changing constantly until successful models are developed.

This is a very natural process for start-ups and their people. It is a very exciting time for those with the stomach to handle the uncertainty. As of this writing, the company described in this chapter has missed several payrolls, but there is a very strong commitment to the concept's ultimate success. No one has left. People have lost their credit rating. In some cases, homes are being foreclosed, and still no one has left. This is a level of making a difference that in my experience only happens when a group of people come together to make a major change in an industry.

The company, in partnership with a major U.S. company, fixes indoor air. By fixing indoor air, I mean the company improves the cost, quality, and comfort of the indoor environment in homes and small businesses.

Eight months ago, I started by developing the company's vision with the CEO as it applied to the various constituencies—consumers, utilities, governments, the partner company, heating and cooling contractors, employees, and owners. After writing the detailed vision or experience of these various constituents, it was clear that our model was way too complicated. As one executive put it: "Too many moving parts."

We knew at that point that we would have to simplify the business model and the vision, but we needed more experience and feedback before a new, more simplified vision could be developed.

Values are difficult to develop in a start-up situation because values often come from observing the personal values of the leader over time. It is a natural process and, when hurried, tends to produce words rather than actions around values. As a result, some simple, preliminary values were adopted in general, but the values are becoming clearer each day and soon will have to be written and inculcated among the team members.

Goals were set for units sold at 10 per month. A unit is a diagnostic device that enables a skilled heating and cooling contractor to diagnose a home's heating and cooling systems in a very objective way. After the causes of problems are identified, the contractor then makes the necessary repairs.

The company's technology has the potential of dramatically improving the energy efficiency of homes and therefore reducing peak energy demand and use of fossil fuels. It also improves comfort and has the potential of resolving indoor pollution issues. Very little of this ultimate potential was known as little as eight months ago.

This phenomenon of a new innovation might be likened to the first personal computer or any other new innovation. In the beginning, it is rather ugly with limited potential except in the eyes of its inventors.

A unit, at that time, sold for approximately $20,000. The unit is sold to contractors that, in turn, use it to conduct home diagnostics for their customers.

A tracking system was put into place to track sales, and two people hit the road to begin selling. One person worked with the national partner to set up meetings with contractors, and one person presented at the meetings. The sale was to get contractors to sign up for the program. Lots of time could have been put into planning this program, but, under the CustomerCulture process, we decided on action and feedback before spending inordinate amounts of time thinking through every part of the program.

This type of "fire, ready, aim" approach will not work in large companies where early precedents create expectations that cannot be sustained. However, in a start-up situation, there are no major expectations, and it works well assuming complete openness and honesty and engaging customers and suppliers as partners in the process. By engaging them, they become part of the evolutionary process rather than the recipients only. They then take full responsibility for their part in the success or failure and are much more forgiving as the evolutionary process develops.

Each of these beginning meetings was successful in signing up a few contractors. After each meeting, the meeting was reviewed for what worked and what didn't and the presenter's perception of what transpired during the meeting.

One of the early goals was contractor success, and contractors were rated on one of three success levels. The feedback was the number of contractors at each success level with the goal being half of the contractors at Level I and half at Level II, which meant that these contractors were actively using the product and changing the way they did business because of it.

After a couple of months of action/reaction using the CustomerCulture process, company managers realized that the product, by itself, was not enough to make the contractors successful and to ensure a long-term win for all concerned. Company managers were also very clear that this is a close-knit industry and that if contractors were not successful with the product, the company would ultimately fail.

As a result, the company began looking for areas that would improve contractor success.

A one-and-a-half-day meeting was conducted with contractors and industry experts in marketing, systems, sales, and technology—10 people in all. The purpose of the meeting was to develop a contractor success model. The meeting began with all team members wishing about what it would take to succeed using the company's technology and ended with definitive next steps that would be taken by meeting team members to build the recommended model.

Out of all this came three basic concepts involving internal and external marketing and ways to use the technology for the contractor to close more sales and make more money.

During the following four months, these concepts were developed and tested by the contractor members present and presented for feedback to new contractors considering the program for their business.

As these concepts were implemented, we learned that contractors could deploy their current technicians to produce bookings for the diagnostic tests. This worked very well, and many contractors began to close a higher percentage of the business at substantially higher margins.

The culture and vision were now developing around contractor success. Nearly everyone was focused on helping contractors do whatever they needed to do to use the product successfully. This became the same as the beginning Federal Express vision: GET THE PACKAGES. In our case, the vision was contractor success.

Stories began spreading about contractors that had discovered ways to use the technology to close more business and homeowners who had their home air fixed and were far more comfortable. Customers became disciples when they saw their energy bills being cut in half in some cases and when their home comfort got to the levels they expected when they purchased their home.

It wasn't long before this became contagious—among employees and the contractor partners.

Success models were defined and tools developed so that contractors considering signing on to the program could evaluate what it meant for their business. These models began with a simple frustration index for the contractors to look at their industry and their frustrations with it.

People will not change until the pain of change is less than the pain of the status quo.

Therefore, change begins with the pain of the status quo, and that is the level of frustration people feel with where they are. The more frustrated with the status quo, we reasoned, the more they will be willing to change and become part of the revolution in their industry.

It is very interesting that in many start-ups there is a known problem, but an unknown solution. For example, when Federal Express began, people often had a latent need to get things delivered overnight, but, because there was not a reliable way to do it, people generally accepted the reality that the problem could not be solved. Therefore, it is no longer a problem they have a strong motivation to solve.

The same is true of our home comfort systems. We purchase a home to have a more comfortable and healthy environment and not have to give up a huge percentage of our weekly pay for that comfort or health. The facts are that 90% of the homes in America are 60% or less energy efficient and that indoor air pollution is from 2 to 100 times worse than the most polluted cities. In addition, 43% of American homeowners have homes that are uncomfortable during hot and cold seasons.

However, with those facts, people don't have a clear path to resolve the issues, so the issues go to the back of the mind unless there is a major problem: known problem—unknown solution.

The company described here is attempting to revolutionize an industry, so we had to develop a process and a culture to drive change in thousands of small and medium businesses and ultimately millions of homes if we are to be successful.

It is very interesting how people view something depending on their vision and goals. If your goal is making contractor partners successful, anything that comes along is viewed within that context.

For example, the company negotiated an exclusive distributorship with a product that essentially breathes home air. It is about the size of a telephone and hooks up the same way. After it is hooked up to an electrical line and a telephone, it breathes all day long and reports the quality of the air it is breathing to the Internet early each morning.

Essentially, the device is used like canaries used to be used in mines, constantly testing the quality of the environment. At present, children are the canaries that test the quality of the air in most homes because air pollution is 2 to 100 times worse indoors than outdoors.

The product was introduced as simply another product in a line of products to help consumers determine whether their indoor air was polluted or not. It had nothing to do with making our contractor partners successful, but, because the culture was focused on making contractors successful, it was viewed under that light.

Instead of simply adding it to a product line, it was envisioned as the entry into the home and, as such, a way to help contractors gain more customers. After the device identified that a problem existed, the company's diagnostic technology could determine the cause of the problem and could recommend appropriate fixes.

An inexpensive peace-of-mind marketing program targeted at mothers of young children was developed and became the primary thrust for many of the contractor partners to grow their business. When they attended home shows, the AirScan was used as the primary attention getter. Direct mail, radio, TV, and other media were used to entice homeowners to check out the quality of their indoor environment.

This is just one example of how nearly everything the company is doing is directed at contractor success—which means homeowner success.

The philosophy gradually morphed into an analogy of the aircraft carrier described in Chapter 10. We began to see our contractor partners as the jet airplanes on the deck and began communicating with them in that manner—as partners with common customers (homeowners). We no longer saw contractors as customers to be sold and supported, but rather as partners with a common vision of reaching out to homeowners.

We implemented a feedback system from them so that we knew their success level and set up a consulting organization to physically go out and work with them to succeed.

As we went back to our original vision, the business model became much simpler. We saw contractor success as the model. If utilities, our major partner, or anyone else could help us achieve that vision, we would use that leverage, but we didn't attempt to serve all constituencies as equal. The customer was the consumer. Our joint (contractor and company) focus is on delivering value to the homeowner.

Contractor success meant consumer acceptance. The facts were clear. Indoor air pollution was "the distant murmur of need that will become the crescendo of a market," to quote Fred Smith.

We envisioned a concept called EvianAir to describe the vision— air that was guaranteed to be healthy. We continue to imagine restaurant windows, motel rooms, and homes all with EvianAir inside. Whether it ends up as EvianAir or some other kind of air is irrelevant to the vision. The vision of clean, healthy air in millions of homes is the all-pervasive vision for the company.

This was a much simpler vision. The values followed suit. The critical value was contractor success. The story became simple and much-needed financing became easier to acquire.

Everything is changing around this vision. The marketing support systems for the contractor, the contractor enrollment process, and nearly everything else we do is in support of the vision.

For example, the contractor enrollment process (formerly the sales process) changed dramatically. The former process was for contractors to come to a meeting, sign up for training involving the owner and a technician, go to training for both the business model and learning how to use the technology, and then decide whether or not to purchase.

The new model is to come to a meeting and sign up for a one-day Quantum Growth Seminar designed to show contractors how to succeed with the new enabling technology offered by the company. Then they decide to join and send their technician to training on how to use the equipment and sell to the homeowner with it.

Instead of selling technology to contractors, we now engage contractors in a business success model called the HomeScan Business System. We even developed an Internet-based technician profiling system to enable our contractor partners to evaluate the technicians they have chosen to enroll in the technician training program.

As we moved to a vision of contractor success, contractor partners got far more serious about the use of the technology to revolutionize the way that they conduct business. We got stories of higher consumer close rates and higher margins on the sales to homeowners. Contractors were ready to increase their commitment to the program and, as a result, wanted us to limit the number of contractors in a given market. We responded by limiting the number of contractors at least for one year in each Metropolitan Statistical Area (MSA).

Using this limit, the whole sales mindset has begun to change around how contractors are approached. In the beginning, we approached them with a mindset of having to convince the contractor to join the program. We had to sell the network to contractors.

Now we approach the contractors with a revolutionary new business system that will, on average, double their revenues and triple their profits. We will be enrolling only X number of qualified contractors in your area for this breakthrough business system, and we will be accepting enrollments on a first-come, first-served basis. If you're interested, please come to learn more about it or come to our Quantum Growth Seminar.

Compare that offer to "We have breakthrough technology to diagnose homes. You can purchase this technology for $22,000."

Other innovation needs were made apparent under the contractor success vision. At every contractor meeting, the frustration index was used to help contractors stand back from their business and take a more objective look at their frustrations. Those frustrations helped us define the issues in the industry that we might be able to help with.

One such frustration that always ranked high was the inability to recruit and keep high-performing technicians. We developed a system using the laptop computer that comes with our equipment to both propose the homeowner repairs needed and to be able to partner with an industry supplier to pay technicians by the job, similar to the way this is done in the automotive industry.

If you have a brake job done on your 1997 Ford Explorer, there is a flat rate dealers pay their mechanics. We developed the same system for contractors so that they could pay for performance. That meant that, by joining our alliance, they could attract and keep high-performing employees because they could afford to pay them far more than averages, based on their performance.

All of this is in eight months, and it's growing every day. Contractors now are beginning to consider it a privilege to join our alliance.

This chapter simply provides an example of innovation in action driven by a vision and CustomerCulture that has changed over time from being multiconstituency centered to being customer (homeowner) centered and partnering with contractors to succeed in delivering EvianAir to those customers.

Let's look back at the CustomerCulture process that was implemented to achieve this level of successful innovation. In this case, the vision gradually (in eight months) went from a very complex too-many-people-groups-to-serve to a much simpler make the contractor successful.

It is especially important to keep the vision simple during a start-up.

Very simple things in existing companies become incredibly complex during a start-up venture. The reason for this is that every change, no matter how small, introduces a change in habits. When lots of simultaneous changes are going on, it is very difficult for people to change several habits simultaneously.

In an existing company, a simple change to a form may require the people who use and process that form to change, but it doesn't change beyond that. Consider changing an enrollment form that is driven off how contractors are enrolled, what the business offer is, and with only a couple of days to pull it all together, and you begin to understand the complexity of interacting habits.

After our vision became increasingly clear, all kinds of innovative processes, forms, technologies, and so forth, were developed around that contractor success vision.

In the meantime, goals were set with the feedback system in place to constantly review what was working and what was not. This led to the change in vision and many more powerful innovations during the company's start-up period.

These innovations continue because now the CustomerCulture supports innovation as the routine way of doing business.

We will revolutionize the Heating, Ventilating, and Air Conditioning (HVAC) industry and change the way people in North America think about their indoor environment.

## CHAPTER 17

ANATOMY OF A TURNAROUND: CUSTOMER CULTURE IN TRANSITION

Frank Chamberlain is a turnaround CEO. He is generally hired by the board of directors of troubled companies to come in and get the business profitable. He is a hired gun.

He has been doing this for 25 years and has headed 19 companies in this role as a turnaround executive.

Most turnaround experts go in with a very sharp scalpel and cut fast and close. They are generally hired to do the dirty work and get rid of most of the people, bring the company to a Spartan existence, and then recruit a new team and revitalize it.

In short, they are meant to stop the bleeding and heal the company. Unfortunately, in most cases, the employees and management left behind are decimated, and it generally takes three years to rebuild the company into a profitable entity, assuming it can be done at all. Often, the assumption is that all the people there caused the problem and therefore none of them have much value in the turnaround—particularly the executives.

This is a high-risk business and most turnaround executives fail at it at least part of the time, but are successful enough to make it worthwhile for troubled companies and their boards.

Frank Chamberlain is an exception and, in many ways, legendary.

Frank's approach is simple and different. The key word is **trust**. He begins by building a culture of trust so that people trust each other and their leaders. Then he trusts the people to actually accomplish the turnaround.

Frank takes a CustomerCulture approach. He believes that when you get your culture right, all else follows, and he backs up this philosophy with action—and results. He has worked with 19 separate companies and has not failed yet. His story demonstrates the power of cultural structures and customer focus in what most would consider impossible situations.

His current turnaround is a midsized company with 14 offices in the home services business. When he took on the responsibility, there were 700 employees. Today, nine months later, there are 600. If not handled correctly, that kind of right-sizing demoralizes the remaining people, making it even more difficult to get to profitability.

Think about the company in need of a turnaround manager.

Its employees are emotionally burned out after years of struggle and failure. Generally, the best employees have already left. The remaining employees are uncertain, distrustful, and scared. Trust in leadership at this point is nonexistent. People have already been told all the hopeful stories about how the company is going to do better only to find out time after time that management has not been truthful or realistic.

In Frank's current turnaround, there were large financial losses over the previous two years and the board explored the consulting services of a bankruptcy attorney who recommended Frank and his organization.

Ten months after Frank began, the company is now profitable with great prospects for a very profitable future. Again, Frank has been there for 10 months, not three years.

I have met three of his executives and they are as optimistic and aggressive as a company that has been enormously successful and just come off another banner year. According to them, the morale in the company has never been higher and they are looking forward to a banner year this year. Hope and trust are back—this time in reality.

Other turnarounds I have witnessed are totally broken at this point in the turnaround process with an uphill battle in front of them and the people are tired, burned out, and definitely not very excited.

Frank's current company and the 18 others he has led are obvious exceptions.

You might ask, "Why use a turnaround company as an example of CustomerCulture thinking?" The answer is that the principles Frank uses will work anywhere. The reality is that even if your company as a whole doesn't require a turnaround expert, at some point individuals, departments, and portions of companies always need turnaround thinking and acting.

This chapter addresses how Frank creates this type of amazing turnaround without totally demoralizing the company and its people, and in fact building a strong foundation and extraordinary success.

Frank had received a call in the fall of 2000 from one of the board members who had been referred by the bankruptcy attorney. At that point he was unavailable and recommended another executive who went into the company and completed a cash flow analysis.

Frank's engagement at that time ended in early February 2001. As he did with every transition from one engagement to another, he went on vacation. When he returned he had a message from the same director from the troubled company wanting to know his present situation.

The board had already removed the chief executive, chief operating, and chief financial officers of the company. The company was under the gun as there was no one to steer the ship. Frank got the call on Thursday, met with the board on Friday, and began his engagement the following Monday. This is typical in these situations.

As you might expect, Frank found a very demoralized group of employees. They lacked strategic direction, there was a great deal of anxiety among the general managers of his remote offices, and there was enormous skepticism on the part of all employees. Management had lost its credibility.

As a company begins to go downhill, all kinds of dynamics come into play. Generally, key managers closet themselves and go within, further cutting off communications. Employees always imagine the worst and there is a very active grapevine. Every change, no matter how small or positive, is viewed as another notch in the gun of a management team that no longer cares about its people. It becomes a very "me" culture with every person, no matter what level, looking out for themselves.

Frank's comments upon going into a new engagement:

"Here is what I find. The company is always disorganized and confused. People are scared. The best employees have left the company, and the remaining employees are upset, suspicious, and anxious. Suppliers have not been paid. Customers are hearing the rumors because competitors are spreading them. Everyone is firefighting. No plans are being followed. The first task is always convincing distrusting suppliers and employees not to leave. This is the generic atmosphere that I run into, and this company was no exception."

The first thing Frank does is tell the employees what they already know and what management is continuing to deny. He tells them the whole truth and doesn't varnish it or sugarcoat it in any way. He lays it out exactly as it is. His assumption is that people are adults who want and can tolerate the truth. What they cannot handle is mistrust and uncertainty. They want trusted leaders and those are leaders who keep them informed.

If there is one secret that Frank conveys, it is to build and deserve the trust of the people. And then he trusts those people to know their business and accomplish the change in direction. Frank does this with absolute honesty and the passionate adherence to giving people the permission to be honest in return, as you'll soon see.

One example of this was one of Frank's previous turnarounds. He was asked by the board to help, and they said they would remove the existing CEO. Frank, after reviewing the CEO's credentials, asked the board to hold off for seven weeks.

One of the executives with this company at the time comments, "We knew we were in trouble. We were like battered children protecting the parent. The existing president kept telling us things were going to get better. In fact, when he introduced us to Frank on his first day as a consultant, he painted a rather rosy picture."

After listening to the president tell his executive team how good things were, Frank got up and commented that the president had not told the whole truth. He then went on to paint a very bleak picture.

The executive team had two responses. First, it felt that there was going to be a battle at the top for power, and it was clear that Frank was going to challenge this man. But, as one of the executives said, "We got the truth that we already knew. All of a sudden, we began to believe that the light at the end of the tunnel might not be a freight train. At least that was our hope. There was still a wait-and-see attitude, but Frank had begun immediately to gain our trust."

You must meet Frank personally to understand his success. His ego is not in charge. He does not do what he does for power—just the opposite. He is in absolute integrity. His actions follow his words. His actions follow his commitments in the smallest of details.

Again, he is building trust in all that he does. If he says a meeting will start at 8 a.m., it starts promptly at 8. If he takes a 10-minute break, his return is prompt. According to Frank, these little commitments demonstrate a very simple principle, "When you say you will do something, do it. Performance against commitments is essential to trust." Everything you do is to earn trust and to identify the people you can trust to get you to profitability.

This comment reminded me of a Ghandi story. I had met a woman who once worked with Ghandi in his effort to free India from British rule. Decades after Ghandi's death, although most meetings in India started well after their appointed time, this woman would always show up on time and would wait quite a while before the meeting got under way.

Once she was asked why she always came on time if she knew the meeting would start much later. She responded, "We once had a meeting with Ghandi and we were late. When the meeting did get started, our leader very calmly and quietly, but with great presence, said, 'If we can't meet our commitment to each other to come together on time, what makes us believe we have the commitment necessary to kick the British out of India?'"

She went on to say that from that point on, meetings started and ended on time, and Ghandi was able to accomplish the impossible by breeding trust at a very foundational level.

Trust, as we all know, is a very fragile thing. It doesn't come from the big things, but rather the thousands of small things that demonstrate to people that we mean what we say and that our actions reflect our meaning. We are in integrity.

Frank's comment is that the first thing you have to understand is that the CEO is always the problem. No matter what problems are found, it is the CEO who caused them. After the seven weeks, Frank recommended the removal of this particular CEO.

Frank described the CEO's style and results, "What he had created was fear—bullying was his method. He tended to be hot-tempered and reduced ladies to tears. He led by fear and was always gilding the lily and glossing over the real problems that troubled the company. He was a poor listener and did not solicit ideas."

Frank begins every engagement with his diagnostic process to define the issues.

This is a process that can and should be used in any department or company where there are significant issues needing correction. I have described it here in-depth as it is the type or process that can be used by any good facilitator—a leader with the desire to accomplish objectives without the need for the perceived power that comes from ordering people around.

The diagnostic process begins by selecting 14 people who are representative of the organization. For a company, these people would represent all critical functions and all levels of the organization. If the company is large, there may be several meetings. In his latest engagement, Frank had nine meetings in all—two at the corporate office and seven from the field offices.

The meetings last from one to two days depending on the nature of the group. If it is a field office, the meetings will last one day. Corporate executives will meet for two days. The executive meeting is held at the end of the process.

Frank starts recruiting for the diagnostic sessions by talking to managers first. He asks questions about each potential candidate as part of the diagnostic. The ideal people do their jobs well, but tend to be curious about activities that go beyond their immediate responsibility. The second quality he looks for tends to be people who have courage and willingness to speak out. It is essential to select people who represent each of the functional activities at that site and people at different levels of the organization. His goal is to x-ray the department or company and that means people with peripheral vision who know what is going on and can provide x-ray-type insight.

He assembles the people in the room and begins by creating an environment of total candor. The meeting starts and ends promptly. There is no expressed judgment allowed. People are allowed and encouraged to tell all that they know or perceive. Openness is recognized as a positive contribution.

Frank begins by explaining the rules and has people take a few moments to get in touch with their feelings—emotionally, how do they feel about being here? He writes those feelings on the flipchart, and they invariably come down to people feeling "uncomfortable and anxious—not knowing what to expect."

He then has people take some time to write down a list of 8- to 10-word headlines that define what he calls a Potential Improvement Point (PIP) in their organization.

Then he starts with the first person and asks the person to state his or her headline and then talk about the issue. The headline is written on a flipchart. When the first person is through, he or she turns and passes the right to speak to the person seated to the right using his or her name in the process. During this time, no one is allowed to speak except the person who has the floor. Frank, as facilitator, may ask questions designed to get as much information out as possible.

This process continues for several hours round and round the room until everyone's list has been exhausted.

At this stage of the diagnostic, it is important not to have the people talk about solutions, but simply to define the problem (PIP) as clearly as possible. Frank is very clear about what an improvement is: "It is a statement of what is missing or what is present that is holding us back." He wants only what exists today and not the solution at this stage of the process. Most people want to start with a solution. He starts with what exists and what is missing that is undesirable. Frank wants PIPs for anything that is "under our control."

There is no such thing as discussion or talking of any kind. You sit there and you listen. Magical things happen. First, when you know you can't talk, you listen. This is the first time that most people don't have to worry about being interrupted. They determine when they're finished. When people are listening, you speak at greater depth and take more personal risks. This diagnostic system also takes the blame out of the issues. You simply state what is without blame or responsibility.

At the end of this session, the headlines are written on 3 × 5 index cards and categorized to common issues, and the reality of where the organization is as a whole comes out. Generally, two issues invariably come to the top as causal factors—lack of trust and lack of communication. Everyone begins to see the trend of what is going on.

Participants often don't understand the subtle things the facilitator does. The important thing in this process is to create a climate where people are free to speak the truth. This portion of Frank's process requires a skilled facilitator and is the core of everything he brings to the organization—create a climate where people are free to speak the truth and then act on it.

The facilitator cannot have a stake in the causes of the issues being presented. If the facilitator has been running the company, she or he will not be open to hear the facts and therefore will shut down the participants.

In Frank's words, there are other very important facilitator tips: "We start precisely on time. We break on time. I'm teaching commitment. We make a game out of it when someone violates the rules. We set up a system to provide feedback. This is usually a $1 penalty for a violation, and I appoint a person to administer the game. We usually collect from $18 to $30. This person is also the timekeeper who enforces the rules."

He also appoints another person to give an overview of the emotional dynamics of the group from time to time throughout the day. The experience is an emotional roller coaster for the participants, and Frank wants them to realize that this experience is normal and acceptable.

After the categorization of the PIPs, Frank breaks the group up into smaller teams to develop and present recommended solutions.

Frank asks each person to comment on his or her feelings at the end of the day. At this point, the feelings are invariably positive.

The process itself is magical. Those simple rules and good facilitation tend to produce mutual respect. Frank points out that his belief in the process and principles of participation and speaking the truth is so strong that he has impact because of his feelings about it. Again, he is in complete integrity with the process.

The "feelings observer" is there to make people aware of what is going on in the room. This runs the gamut from people feeling uncomfortable stating the unsayable to the highs of laughter and understanding. Frank wants people to see that it is not only OK to express feelings, opinions, and perceptions, but preferred. It is their truth.

In the beginning, people generally don't know what to expect and feel nervous. At the end of the day, the first building block to honesty and trust is established. The overwhelming message is: We will listen to and want the truth as you see it.

The process allows two hours to develop the action plans and present them back to the overall group. The group is then free to critique, edit, and argue these plans. The action plans are tested in front of the whole group.

According to Frank and his people, the process alone isn't what makes it work—it's the facilitator. When an organization gets in trouble, everyone clams up. The overriding issue is lack of trust, and nothing short of total honesty and being trusting of others can resolve this issue.

Generally, there has already been too much ego and not enough listening in the organization. This process gets people talking and listening.

The most important ingredient in Frank's overall process is integrity. It is doing what you say you're going to do. It is honest dealing. It is speaking truth.

The essential point that Frank makes is, "Integrity is the one and only thing that over time any group will respect."

Many have argued with Frank that this is naïve on his part, but his results and stubborn adherence to building the culture of integrity proves the process not even worthy of argument.

This is the essence of the whole process. Inconsistency loses trust and credibility. You cannot afford to lose credibility. You have shell-shocked people looking for lack of integrity. They need a leader and an environment that restores trust.

A culture of integrity is also a quality environment where Frank has little problem attracting high-performing executives even though the risk of turnaround is legendary.

It's quite simple. People want to work hard and be respected. If you can demonstrate to them that the culture supports hard work and respect, they want to be part of it, often without regard to risk.

One executive recruited for two different turnarounds said that her mother thought she was crazy. She commented, "I know the environment that Frank creates. I will work hard and be appreciated."

After several months, there is an environment of cooperation. People went from darts to kudos in the analysis of their contribution. The result is a higher level of performance. People are proud to be there. People hold their heads high and believe that the company is a good place to work.

This result is beginning to be strongly felt by this company's competitors. Instead of spreading rumors of the company's demise, they are strangely silent and, I suspect, afraid.

Most of the company's key managers are new people and strong players. Several layoffs occurred and were dealt with very carefully. Everyone saw the numbers. People knew they were not efficient. There were no big surprises.

How do you get through repeated layoffs? Business leaders that have had to go through waves of layoffs always want to do it once and have it done, but this is impractical so it is done in waves. To answer the question, you communicate. You tell people why. You share information. You always talk about reality. If it makes sense to you, you simply talk about it openly. If you've carried this off in the past, they know you're telling the truth.

The company's vice president of human relations expresses another one of Frank's philosophies: "Every employee comes with a mind that costs nothing extra. We need to remember that. In this organization, people are now using their minds."

The company has a new management team, it has re-staffed, and it is profitable with exceptionally high morale. There is optimism among the people. The company no longer has a recruiting problem. Managers are constantly approached by people who want to join the company. It has a budget, and there are no fairytales. It is getting closer and closer to hitting the budget and meeting its goals.

It is focused on training and getting all of its people to higher and higher performance.

The company just presented its budgets to its board and bank and it is profitable—the first year since this rollup began in 1998.

One of the board members commented, "Before we brought Frank on, we asked an investment banker to come in and were told to plan on a three-year undertaking to get to profitability. We've had a wonderful experience with the turnaround team—a totally unexpected experience."

As Frank says, "We focus on soft discipline—integrity and trust. Your people will tell you what the problems are and how to solve them. For some reason, most executives don't understand the importance of this very basic truth or how to listen long enough to improve their organization and themselves.

"One of the big secrets of turnarounds is that the problem is always the CEO. After you understand that, it manifests itself in different ways. Usually, but not always, the CEO tends to use an autocratic style of leadership, makes all the decisions, and views people as tools to implement his or her ideas.

"The moment you begin to think that way you turn people off. You can get their thinking free, but with an autocratic style, you create fear and unknowingly teach people to hold their tongue and remain safe within their shell."

Frank wants them to "tell me when I'm doing the dumb. Argue with me."

The autocrat doesn't want to hear that. He or she wants employees to be passive and certainly not proactive. The autocrat's thinking is, "certainly you don't want employees to exercise their own judgment. They're not as smart or they don't know the business as well as I do."

One of the reasons that companies get in trouble is that the authoritarian style diminishes the effect of their employees. Competitors that are more enlightened drive these companies into failure.

One of Frank's advantages is that he generally knows little or nothing about the business and must trust experienced employees. Frank feels so strongly about people's desire to serve and meet goals that he sincerely seeks their ideas. He wants their participation. He sets up formal processes to ensure they are informed and listened to. He invites disagreement. He wants you to tell him when he's wrong. People must learn to speak the truth as they see it, which is unusual for many cultures.

One might expect employees to take advantage of the perceived power Frank gives them, but according to Frank, there are no downsides. People don't abuse it. You will always find individuals that are the exceptions, but their peers quickly call it in an open environment.

"I want people to feel free to challenge. I want people to take their stand and listen to others take their stand and then argue it out. I want people to feel secure enough in who they are to be themselves. Our cultural process creates the freedom for people to be and express who they are."

Now, let's go back to the CustomerCulture system.

1. Vision: The overriding objective (and vision) is to become profitable. We will do everything possible to become profitable. And all are responsible. The vision might be stated, "Profitable together in an environment of integrity."

2. Values: Integrity, honesty, openness, delegation, decentralization. The values stress power in the hands of the employees led by leaders who understand the power of dedicated people with a clear purpose. A value violation is a withhold of the truth, a lack of openness, or a lack of integrity.

3. Goals: Living the values (employee), financial performance (owner), and customer satisfaction (customer).

4. Relevance: Frank makes achieving the goals relevant to his people in the usual ways with one twist. He makes sure they are listened to and given a sense of control over their

own destiny. This type of cultural structure invariably creates relevance.

5. Feedback: Feedback is everywhere. Once you have established honesty and openness, everything is out there. Although the organization needs some objective and numeric feedback, everyone becomes a coach. Peers give each other feedback. Managers feel they can be openly honest with a low-performing employee. That said, there is a scoreboard at Frank's company. It is simple and effective because it is backed with the subjective feedback that comes from honest human relationships.

6. Accountability: This is essential in Frank's process. People are given the trust and the responsibility, but they must perform. There are no excuses, and each person is held accountable.

7. Actions: It is clear that delegation goes as far down the organization as people are ready to accept it. Frank is the best example. He knows nothing about the industry. He simply gets people to be honest and open, and they do it all. This permeates throughout the organization.

The following is an example of Frank's diagnostic and action process in action when it comes to serving customers.

At the diagnostic sessions, a PIP was identified as the telephone system. It had been automated with customers and employees getting bounced around in voicemail jail. The diagnostic pointed to many customers who were upset with the phone system.

The company ended up answering the phone with a person and putting customer service, service technicians, dispatch, and everyone who dealt directly with customers in a well-designed bullpen (see the Single Egg Organization). This type of customer-centric organization puts people in an environment where customer needs are constantly met with little direction needed from management.

Frank is a skeptic when it comes to policy manuals. He believes much more strongly in communicating, listening, and living these values by example. You spell out how you want things done, and it is much more effective.

"I hired Judy. She lives and breathes these same values. I'm saying that I intuitively believe that people will learn to do things from watching others much more effectively than by reading a piece of paper. Policy manuals are substitutes for on-the-spot coaching and living the values. And they often get in the way."

Frank goes on to say, "The older I get, the more important I believe having fun at work is. I see that it is so easy to unintentionally destroy the morale of people. Managers are perceived to be much more powerful than they believe they are. People must have joy and fun in their jobs to give you lasting productivity, and it is the leader's job to build that fun and productive environment.

"I have fun every day. I love what I do. I have fun because I feel free to do the things that I want to do and in the way that I want to do them. I want to create a climate that is fun and informal. I want people to be themselves so they have the same freedoms that I do."

As a postscript to this last issue of having fun and making the job fun for others, I was in the Big Brothers program for seven years and my little brother was Mark. In fact, Mark is now 24 and he works with me today.

I'll never forget picking him up one Saturday when he was about seven years old and asking if he was having a good day.

"Yes, I'm having a great day," came the reply.

I asked him, "So what's the difference between a good day and a bad day for you?"

"That's simple. A good day is when I get to do what I want to do, and a bad day is when I'm doing what my mother, my teacher, and others want me to do."

Such wisdom from a seven-year-old.

One might easily make the statement, "If we let everyone do what they wanted to do, we would have anarchy."

After being involved with many companies that follow the principles in this book, my answer is always, "You'd be surprised. Empowered people with a clear purpose and direction will always go further to serve their customers and make you a profit than you could ever ask them or tell them to."

And I've never seen an exception to that simple statement.

THE VISION OF THE IDEAL AT A FEDERAL EXPRESS STATION

The idea of vision is to describe in detail what the organization is to accomplish if it is to be successful. It is a written description of what the various stakeholders will experience in a successful company.

The following vision was written by me in 1978 as Federal Express was gaining major momentum in the marketplace. The company was doubling every year, and this growth was hiding many problems that this vision addressed.

The vision is shown as an example for those leaders who desire to get very clear about what their organization is to accomplish. The topics covered are obviously very specific to Federal Express.

The concept of a detailed description of the experience of the various constituencies (customers, employees, owners, and suppliers) is as applicable today as it was in 1978.

Federal Express had developed a plan entitled Basics, Business, and Cost, allowing three months of a fiscal year for the specific change of focus for each. This was a top-down effort that needed reinforcing at the station (local pickup and delivery operation) level, which prompted the writing of this vision.

This type of vision can be written by any manager interested in building and achieving a vision of success for his or her department, division, or company.

My function at the time was the senior vice president of the southern division. As a result of this vision and the goals, relevance, and feedback that accompanied it, the division was able to rise from ranking three and four in every feedback category to one and two in those same categories by the end of one year.

This vision was published in the company newspaper exactly as shown next.

THE FEDERAL EXPRESS STATION: AN IDEAL

During the first half of this year we have changed focus twice—first basics, then volume. Now we are changing again, this time to cost.

Why keep changing focus? We're not. Or at least that is not our intent. Our intent is to build: Basics—the foundation, Business—the walls, Cost—the roof. A conscious plan to build your station into a satisfying place to work where winning is second nature and people can freely express themselves. Where solving the customer's problem is something we do because we want to and where everyone, our people as individuals, our people as a company and our customers, receives a fair return for what is given. In other words: People, Service, Profit (the company's value system).

But all this can be confusing when we know we're up to it in alligators. First this priority, then that one. Service goes down, we complain. You add people, cost goes up, and we complain again.

We might ask, "What do you want from me? Perfection?" My answer is "yes": perfection in the sense of growing towards an ideal. The following is an attempt to paint a picture of the ideal station, not perfect in the sense of making no mistakes—we're all human—but ideal in the sense of winning the game—a picture that attempts to consider all aspects of the business as I now see it, and as I see it for the future.

THE IDEAL STATION

Our People—Our people are free to express themselves—their likes and dislikes towards each other and towards the company as a whole. When it comes to the customer, they care enough to want to solve the problem and let our customer know it. We'll make a mistake but if we care enough we can correct it and work to see that it doesn't happen the next time.

Our people are honest in the sense of not promising more than they can do, but often doing more than is promised. They live up to their commitments to others, and if they can't, they simply don't commit.

The ideal station has an attitude that is hard to express. People who don't mind quarreling among themselves, but when the chips are down, which they often will be, there is a team spirit that would have made Custer's last stand into the first of many more to come.

Our Service—Our on-time delivery is consistently at 95% or better regardless of the obstacles. If the plane is late, we recover. If it's constantly late, we try to find out why and change it. If we can't change it, we accept it and solve the problem by re-thinking the operation. We don't worry about who caused the failure, because our customers don't care. They just want what we promised them. If we give it to them, we'll get their business. If we give them excuses, they'll find competitors who are just as good at giving excuses. Our job is to solve the customers' problem.

We treat every customer contact as we would want to be treated. When we call someone, we would like to be treated with dignity and respect—meaning that the phone is answered promptly and courteously by someone who cares enough to listen and move to solve the problem—by someone who is not satisfied until every problem has been solved and every package has found its place—by someone who takes the responsibility, makes the commitment and sees to it that each personal commitment is kept—by someone who has become Federal Express in "their" customer's eyes.

I'll never forget the customer who was asked, "What do you do when you have a problem with Federal Express?" He spontaneously replied, "I call Debbie. She is Federal Express."

The ideal station treats each new problem as a challenge, a winning situation—not an excuse, a chance to blame others, to lose.

Our Profit—The ideal station doesn't treat profit as an end, but rather as a means to an end—a way to grow, a way to attain a higher standard of living, a way of providing more jobs—jobs that are not make-work because we want to cover every potential challenge, but rather jobs that have the challenge of life—jobs that require ideas, decisions and actions—jobs that provide expression to each individual in each of these areas with the result being the positive feelings of a job well done.

Profit to an ideal station considers two distinct areas: revenue and cost.

Revenue is created by providing good service and telling people about it. Doing one without the other is like talking without listening or vice versa.

The ideal station, then, considers our station people an integral part of sales and our sales people an integral part of our station. They are one and inseparable—just different people doing different jobs for the same end. Perceived structural lines which separate sales and station are simply excuses for people who would rather blame others instead of taking responsibility for their own future and their own success. A football team has a very complicated structure to develop and make the players ready. Once they're in the game, however, it's a team with each doing his own part with none worrying who they'll catch hell from between this game and the next.

The second part of profit is cost. How many times have we heard, "He runs a tight ship"? That's what we're talking about, not using people and not being used by people. The goal is a well-thought-out operation, planned to meet our people's needs and satisfy our customer's problems at minimum expense.

I do not mean to imply that it's right to go easy on people. "Going easy" generally means giving a person only part of our feelings. It's easy for some people to express just positives and for others to express just negatives. Neither works. The only way that works is to express what we really feel. Many textbooks recommend expressing a positive before a criticism. I agree with the action, but not with the implications of being false or phony. The positive must be real or the total expression has no value. Search for what you like and don't like, then express it—all of it.

Many times we demand perfection from ourselves, but hesitate to ask our fellow employees for the same. That is an injustice to ourselves and to our partners. Caring is giving. Giving is the full expression of ourselves to another. If we demand quality from ourselves, we really want it from others. Why not ask for it? Are we afraid? The ideal station has the courage of expression.

The ideal station watches its costs with a constant assault to cut waste. It searches to find better ways to apply itself, its equipment, and its time to meet our people/service/profit objectives more efficiently. It guards with stubborn vigil the assets entrusted to it. It wants complete openness to confront what is good and bad, for in everything there is both. It seeks to explore and apply new ideas that will improve upon the weaknesses.

The ideal station lets people know where they are—both positive and negative. It provides information and performance evaluations to individuals so that they may have the opportunity to see themselves from another's perspective and grow in the process, and so that they can better play their part in meeting the station's goals.

Regarding cost, the ideal station makes a definite cost commitment based on achieving well-understood goals and objectives. Like all commitments, it accepts nothing less than fulfilling these commitments without compromising our people or our service. And, the ideal station never allows itself to get caught in that compromise, except temporarily.

Our Work Place—The ideal station recognizes the need for cleanliness and organization in order to provide each individual the ability to live up to his or her own potential. It recognizes that our customer's primary buying motive is trust. And that trust must be earned by providing consistent service, personal involvement and a very real image of people and systems that respond to that need.

Our environment, whether it is in the office, our vans, the uniform with a name tag or any number of other seemingly small details creates this image. It is as fundamental to our business as exercise is to a football team. It helps us to be proud and ready to meet the challenges that will come. It creates the atmosphere that allows us to respond in a clear, problem-solving way. The organized work place cuts down on confusion and resulting errors that could affect our people or our service. The ideal station then provides a clean and organized work place, not because it has to but because it is part of its nature.

Our Interface—Finally, the ideal station team members realize that their station is not an island. It is part of a system—a greater team of individuals who need certain things in order to do their part—on-time departures, accurate and timely reporting, attention-to-detail at every step.

The ideal station has no tolerance for poor paperwork, missed reports, late departures, incomplete reports, customers not notified, consignees not located, etc. It decides on the front-end that these things will not happen and develops the necessary plans to deliver on its commitments day in and day out—never failing.

When it does fail, which sometimes it must, the station is totally honest admitting the error and moving to correct it. The ideal station talks about what did happen only in the sense that the information helps it solve the problem and not to excuse the occurrence. It recognizes that first-time mistakes will happen, but that second-time mistakes are inexcusable.

Summarizing, the ideal station is a group of people, never perfect, but always growing—never there, but better this week than last with a balanced attack against all barriers which stand in its way—accepting total responsibility for its fate.

We have many ways of evaluating a station against this ideal. Some are very objective and number oriented: volume, revenue, service, cost, audit results. These are excellent indicators of what is, but not necessarily what will be. Some are subjective: people attitudes, customer attitudes, work place organization. These are perceptions that give us an indicator of what the future brings. For example, if a customer has a need to talk to someone outside the station about a problem, generally it means that the people did not care enough to listen and solve the problem. That attitude is gradually conveyed to other customers and our revenue growth begins to slow.

The ideal station is an end and a means, an achievement and a process—the process of growth, of keeping what is positive, accepting what is negative and acting to correct it. The ideal station is a gift to all of those who are part of it—the chance to be ourselves and to grow. The ideal station is the ideal person. Evaluate yourself and your station.

Where do you stand? Where are you going?

POSTSCRIPT

This article was copied for each employee and introduced in sessions at each of the 28 stations in the division. Employees were asked to each read a paragraph and mention briefly what it meant to them. This set the stage for total focus on the vision and its corresponding goals.

B

THE UPS PHILOSOPHY AS STATED BY ITS FOUNDER

The following is from a document reprinted by UPS in 1963 entitled "Determined Men..." This is a compendium of speeches given from 1943 to 1959.

I believe UPS to be one of, if not the most, successful companies of the 20th century. I believe it has made more millionaires than any other company and that it has successfully gone through adversity that would kill lesser companies.

When reading this book that goes back in time to the 70s and, with this appendix, to 1907 to 1957, you might ask, "How is all this relevant today when so much has changed?"

The reality is that, although much has changed, some fundamental things remain the same. What has not changed is how some companies are able to adapt and evolve through all change regardless of what environmental obstacles face their business.

UPS has been in business nearly 100 years. In that time, it has gone through two world wars, the Great Depression, and a major change in demographics that forced it to vacate its original business model to create the enormous power that UPS is today. It has virtually evolved through every challenge thrown at it because it is driven by a very powerful vision, values, and goals. It also has incredibly powerful relevance (ownership and performance pay) and feedback systems.

This ability to adapt to one's environment is what Darwin spoke about when he said that survival does not go to the most powerful, but rather to the most adaptable. This applies to organizations as much as it does to a given species or individual.

Although there are many reasons for UPS's adaptability, I credit its CustomerCulture as the most predominant. Its vision is not an end, but a journey and a way of thinking that has transcended every challenge possible.

Jim Casey founded UPS in 1907. As a 22-year-old industrial engineer working in a remote district, I had the opportunity to ride to a New York airport in a cab with him shortly before he died. At that point, he was retired. During our trip, I got very little chance to ask him questions because he wanted to know about me—my job, my enjoyment, my passion, my family, my view of UPS, and on and on.

I worked with UPS from 1960 to 1968. The following principles expressed by Jim Casey, although excerpted from speeches made over two decades, were not just words. They express leadership views that the company lived through its actions. Further, they are as relevant today as they were in the 50s. For some, they will bring you back to a sense of corporate values that have been forgotten in today's overly busy world.

We gauge corporate success on a number of indexes such as revenues, profits, growth, market share, longevity, employee commitment, and so forth. UPS excels in every one of these traditional measures. The reason it does is because of its CustomerCulture.

Some of Jim Casey's thinking is summarized here from a document published in the early 60s. It goes to the UPS vision and culture, and Jim Casey's thinking is as essential today as it was 40 years ago.

I apologize for the constant use of the masculine only. I did not want to edit in any way. Seeing how a major business leader viewed gender 50 years ago does show how far we have come at least in our use of words when it comes to balancing gender in business.

Some random quotes from Jim Casey follow, along with a complete speech that summarizes his beliefs about business and what it takes to succeed.

QUOTES

"Determined men make conditions—they do not allow themselves to become victims of them. ...Determined men working together can do anything."

"Our horizon is as distant as our mind's eye wishes it to be."

"Know when to make changes and when to hold fast to what is still good."

"An expanding business is the only way to provide opportunities for our people."—1944

"The business is based upon just a few simple principles and policies. To these we have applied practical ideals—not just copybook philosophy, but a sincere desire to do the right thing and do it well."—1945

"We decided that we must find some field and specialize in it. And in doing so—we probably hit upon the most fundamental policy of all."—1945

"Anybody can deliver packages—from the small boy in the neighborhood on up to the most extensive delivery system in the land. The one thing we can have to offer that others will not always have is quality."—1946

"Are we working for money alone? If so, there is no surer way not to get it."—1947

"We must keep our eyes on the distant horizon and at the same time master the day-to-day problems that lie immediately before us. We must be a step ahead in our thinking—never once believing that we have reached perfection in anything. We must be ready to move quickly in any direction to meet new conditions in a progressive world."—1948

"We have a business that offers much, not only to us but to men still unknown."—1948

"Let us get a clear understanding of our objectives. Only then will we be able to map out the highways, and skyways, and byways that will take us there."—1954

"The basic principle which I believe has contributed more than any other to the building of our business as it exists today…is the ownership of our company by the people employed in it."—1955

"We are practical men and not merely dreamers. We know that our dreams and plans won't get very far unless we have the right men to make them realities."

"One measure of your success…will be the degree to which you build up others who work with you. While building up others you will build up yourself."—1945

"Inspiration and enthusiasm are of little value unless they move us to action and accomplishment."—1946

"A man's worth to an organization can be measured by the amount of supervision he requires."—1947

"Don't over-rate yourself. Lean a little the other way—be constructively dissatisfied with yourself—and you'll go further."

"Others will judge you by what they think of the quality and effectiveness of your work—not what you think of it."

"You cannot be successful entirely through your own efforts. All of us, if we are to accomplish anything worthwhile, will do it largely through the help and cooperation of the people who work with us. We must help others help us."—1947

"Within each of us there is a mysterious innate force that drives us onward. It wants us to do better and be better. Call that force conscience, ambition, determination, power of will, or whatever you choose, it constantly whispers in our ears words of advice, stimulation, and encouragement. If you will but heed the voice and utilize that inner power to the limit of its potentialities, nothing on earth can stop your progress."—1947

"As always, our biggest need will be for broad-gauge men who can think beyond the present and apply sound, mature business judgment to whatever conditions we may have to meet. We need men who can do what has never been done before."—1954

"You can't be a big man until you have shown competence as a small man. You can't expect to handle big responsibilities until you have handled small ones."—1958

"Averages don't mean anything. ...The thing to do is to find out what each man is really capable of doing as an individual, and to deal with him as an individual."—1943

"The ideals of our company cannot be carried out from the top alone. They must become a part of the make-up of our entire organization. They must be instilled in the minds of all men, down through the ranks."—1947

"The problem is to assign to each executive those responsibilities which he can handle with as little reliance as possible upon others for the making of decisions which he alone should make, and to coordinate the activities of our whole executive staff so they will work in harmony and with that degree of mutual understanding that was possible when our business was smaller."—1948

"Each unit of operation, whether a department or a station, large or small, should be headed by a man who has the authority and ability to make practically every decision pertaining to the operation of that department or station. The manager should manage completely everything under his jurisdiction and not merely act as an intermediary or agent for someone else who is the real manager."—1948

"A manager should know when not to make a decision—when the nature of the problem is beyond his sphere or when he feels that it requires consideration by someone else."—1948

"The kind of management we try to have in our company must be a living thing. Its precepts must originate in our hearts. I like to think of a Philosophy of Management rather than a plan of management."—1949

"Good management is not just organization. It is an attitude inspired by the will to do right."

"Good management is taking a sincere interest in the welfare of the men you work with. It is the ability to make men feel that you and they are the company—not merely employees of it."

"Good management is your willingness to have and hold the confidence of other men."—1949

"We try to operate a democratic company. In doing this we function under a philosophy of management not common to all businesses of our size. We want to be a living, breathing institution and not a cold, inanimate, impersonal corporation. We try to have a distinctive company personality, and this, necessarily, must be the composite personality of all of us. We try to avoid needless formalities in our relations with each other. We think of each other as individuals and not as mechanical parts of a machine."

"We try to maintain a spirit of mutuality. We depend upon each executive to carry out his responsibilities with a minimum of interference. We trust each executive to do his best because he wants to do it and not because of fear of retaliation if he fails to put forth his best efforts."

"Those are not just words—they are accurate statements of what we really believe to be the right course to follow."—1952

"We are trying to encourage our people to do, in a business that has grown large, what they would do if the business were small and they were solely responsible for its operation."—1958

"Once the people you deal with come to recognize that what you do springs from an honest heart, they will be surprisingly strong in their support for you.

> They will believe what you say.
> They will do what you want.
> They will give you their loyalty.
> They will trust and follow you."

In 1957, Jim Casey delivered a speech at the company's 50-year anniversary Plant Manager Conference. It was delivered in UPS's founding city of Seattle.

This time period was in the middle of a major transition of the company from retail delivery for department stores to wholesale delivery for business-to-business packages. This was a major upheaval from dealing closely with large department stores for local delivery to building a national network of package handling and delivery, starting with local delivery and then tying it all together.

The following is a verbatim copy of that speech.

DETERMINED MEN

As you must know, an endless variety of thoughts not connected with the conference have gone through my mind this week. The visions passing before my eyes have formed a kaleidoscope.

I saw again Seattle as a pioneer city of barely 60,000 people with the center down near the waterfront. On its streets were horses and wagons and people on foot, on bicycles, on cable cars. Here and there were dog-teams drawing sledges, in training for the carriage of supplies of gold-seeker over the ice fields of Alaska.

I saw again the returning soldiers of the Spanish-American War, marching in a parade with veterans of the Civil War no older than some of you today. I returned to 1897 and my fourth grade in school. I recalled the formative years of youth and smiled inwardly at my boyhood hopes and dreams. I relived the events leading up to the beginning of our company and, later, to my first meetings with you.

It has been given to few men to serve a single business for half a century. And of those few I doubt whether another in all the world has experienced the good fortune of having his partners so many fine men as you and the others, living and dead, who have served with me.

Although now only two years short of three score and ten, I still feel too young—or maybe I am too egotistic—to believe that my usefulness to you and to society is at an end. Nevertheless, I am far too old to imagine that I could have another score of years to serve you.

In the long journey to date the most important discovery I made was one that I came upon early.

I found that I could not hope to accomplish anything worthwhile alone. That is not to say that I have lacked self-reliance. But self-reliance and a sincere desire to give full value to the opinions of others have given me confidence that...**anything jointly decided upon would be successful.**

The rest of what I am to say to you tonight could be condensed into that last simple statement, because any account of the experiences of our company can only be a story of the joint efforts of people—not just a few but many people working together, as we have, for the benefit of all. But, to go on, let me once again tell you of a conversation that took place here in Seattle 40 years ago.

At that time two of us sought the business and financial advice of a man named Carstens, whose office was in the Lowman Building at First and Cherry. He was about 55. We were kids. After listening to our opening remarks and asking us a few questions, Mr. Carstens leaned back in his chair, put his feet up on his desk, and went on with the most inspiring talk on the economics of business that I had ever heard. He closed with the words: "Determined men can do anything."

In the light of my experience of 40 years since hearing those words, I would amend them to say:

"Determined men working together can do anything." And now, as I look back, I doubt that even Mr. Carstens, with all his optimism, could have imagined that a company, still so small after 10 years of struggle, could become a national institution of 10,000 men such as we are today. (They are now 400,000 people.)

On the present occasion—the annual Plant Managers' Conference of our now great company, in the city of its birth in the 50th year of its life—it seems fitting that I should recall a few of the experiences we have shared together and express the hope that we will together continue to profit from the lessons learned in all these years.

Everything great is the manifestation of a basic idea, or principle.

When a basic principle is developed by logical thinking, sponsored by integrity and clearly defined, faith in the proposition is almost sure to follow. And where faith is strong enough, almost anything seems possible. Complete faith in certain definite principles is the very foundation of our company—United Parcel Service. Most of the principles, which we like to refer to as company policies, were developed slowly. It is hard to point to any one of them as the product of a single mind. In fact some of our now basic policies are the results of hundreds of hours of thinking and discussion among dozens of men.

Our general policies are so well known to most of you that mere mention of them may seem like unnecessary repetition. Even so, I want to re-emphasize a few. Take our first example, the decision to specialize in a narrowly limited kind of business. Had our chief motive been the gathering in of dollars, that decision would not have been made, because sidelines could easily have brought in more revenue—for a while.

Next, I will say something about the ownership of the company. In its earliest years we tried, unsuccessfully, to induce outsiders to invest their money with us. Later, by definite choice, we decided that stock in our company should not be owned by outsiders.

During the first 15 years there were never more than four partners in the business and the total value of all they had at the end of that time was only a few thousand dollars. It was seen, however, that others should be taken into partnership as the business grew, and in 1922, or thereabouts, stock was issued to a few of the men who are among our partners today. In 1927 about 50 more were given the opportunity to buy stock, and in the 30 years since then stock ownership by the men who manage our company has been widespread.

Employee-ownership is credited by people inside and outside the company with having done more than any other thing towards making our company and our people so notably successful financially and otherwise.

Only once did we deviate from the policy of keeping ownership of the company solely in the hands of our own people. In 1929 we made arrangements with a firm of investment bankers, giving our stockholders cash for their holdings and, in addition, a block of stock in a proposed new corporation which was to supply sufficient capital for expansion as fast as we could grow. Fortunately, as seen when looking back upon it, the arrangement did not work out entirely as contemplated, but it did make available to us more cash capital than could have been accumulated through earnings in many years. Without the added capital secured at that time, we could not have expanded from the Pacific Coast directly to New York, in 1930, and in one jump become the largest retail delivery system in the world.

Four hazardous years after our first entanglement with those outside financial interests and at the very lowest point of the general depression which began in 1929, we recovered for our own people full possession of our company. A man now dead skillfully and safely guided us through that experience with an ownership divided between ourselves and outsiders and we learned in those four years lessons that should never be forgotten.

Now for a word about the use of our capital. Originally and for about half of our company's life we avoided purchases of real estate. We know that if we used any part of our profit to buy real estate there could not be enough left to finance a rapidly expanding delivery business. So we found property owners who would lease to us the space we needed.

Eventually it became possible for us to buy land and erect buildings more suitable for our purposes, and today our investment in real estate represents substantially half the book value of our assets. This real estate, as you know, is held separately under an arrangement planned to give all of us a safe hedge against the risks of failure in the delivery business alone.

In thus tracing the origin and development of a few of our company's policies, I have tried to show how necessary it was to...**recognize and follow certain principles and still not become victims of fixed ideas.**

There were times when we did get off the track. Innumerable costly mistakes were made. During the long span of years here so briefly reviewed, we passed through two world wars, a major financial depression and several smaller ones. Despite human errors, war, depressions and other adversities, and their punishing effect upon our company and people, we have been guided by firmly established principles.

We have made no secret of our policies, but have believed it...**inadvisable to broadcast all our business affairs to the world. We have kept confidential facts and figures pretty close to ourselves, as most prudent people do with their own private affairs. In building this privately owned company for the benefit of all of us, we have found that it pays to mind our own business and just keep on sawing wood.**

There have been no supermen in our company—no star performers to hog the limelight. We have able men—yes—and each of us has been encouraged, without fear of penalties, to be himself. We have recognized that individual personalities are hard to change, so we have permitted them to remain unhidden, even though, in some instances, we wish they could be different.

We have become known to all who deal with us as people of integrity, and that priceless asset is more valuable than anything else we possess.

Notwithstanding all I have said about our ability to meet the problems of transition from the horse and buggy age to the marvelous, modern world of 1957, two things have remained beyond our power to control or change. These are the passage of time and inexorable laws of nature. Many fine men of our company died early. Others served us long and well and have retired. Some of us, still active, are showing the effects of advancing age, and each added year will take an increased percentage of the time left to us.

It is not too soon to think of what our successors may do. We must realize that we cannot dictate or devise the tactics of games to be played against unknown opponents, under unknown rules and conditions of future days. So we must trust that the players on our team of a later day will be at least as capable as ourselves. In actual performance they should do better because they will have as guides the fundamental principles which have been discovered, tested, and proved.

Let us, therefore, be as certain as we can that those fundamentals will be clearly understood and that amendments, when necessary, will be in detail rather than in principle. But how can we be sure there will be no basic, ill-considered, unwarranted, unsuccessful changes in policies that have served us so well? How can our company always remain young, strong, modern, aggressive, forward-looking?

How can we be certain of group security, yet with progress and individual achievement, for the people who will constitute our organization and direct our destinies in later days?

We can do all these, first, by preventing the formation of cliques and by avoiding deep-seated quarrels among ourselves. Second, we can do it by keeping the financial control of our company in our own hands. Third, we can do it by learning all that is useful in the profession of management, while avoiding professional management itself. There should never be need for hired professionals to manage our affairs. Fourth, we can do it by giving unified, undivided support to our leaders—who themselves should be men who really know our business, men we can trust and admire, men who are partners financially and otherwise.

Who will those leaders be? They will be men who now, today, are forging ahead—not spectacularly or with fanfare, but modestly and quietly. They are the plain, simple men who are doing their best on their present jobs with us, whatever those jobs may happen to be. Such men will not fail us when called for bigger things.

It is for them, our successors, to remember that all the glamour, romance and success of our business, at any stage of its existence, must be the product of years resulting from the work of many devoted people, and there can be no glamour, no romance, no truly great success, unless shared in by all.

INDEX

Page numbers ending in "f" refer to figures.

95% rule, 162, 244

A

Abraham, Jay, 136
accountability, 85, 238, 248
action
    Federal Express and, 164–65
    feedback to, xxiii, 13, 100
    goals and, 24–28
    turnarounds and, 238
    weekly feedback report, 97–103
advertising, 135–37
airline delays, 143–45
airline security, 148–49
appreciation, 234–35
assumptions, 210–11
authoritarian styles, 236
automating functions, 147
awards for value, 58

B

balanced goals, 128–29
Bell Sports, 159
bottom-line goals, 65, 67
brainstorming sessions, 134, 135
Building the Happiness Centered Business, xxv
business, happiness-centered, xxv, 193, 201–3

C

Casey, Jim
    quotes from, 254–58
    speech from, 258–65
    on success, 253–65
cause-and-effect systems
    cultural structures and, 15–16, 22, 24–28, 25f
    example of, 30–32
    weekly feedback report, 97–103
CEOs, 152, 152f, 229–30
Chamberlain, Frank, 224–40
change, dynamics of, 172–87
    aloneness, 174, 182
    balancing attitudes, 175
    comfort, 174, 182
    creative problem solving, 174–75
    dealing with, 176–81
    exercise for, 172–76
    experiencing, 173
    Federal Express and, 177–80
    handling change, 174, 182–85
    negativity, 174, 175, 182–83
    outside influence, 174, 176
    problem solving, 183–84
    procedures, 182–83
    readiness levels, 174, 175, 183
    resources, 174, 175, 183–84
    in start-ups, 215, 221
change, implementing, 126, 127
changes, dealing with, 131–39

channel-dependent companies, 132, 138
channel network, 135
channel partners, 132–34, 138–39
checks and balances, 126
cleanliness, value of, 47, 48, 55, 247
clients, choosing, 197–98
cobranding Web sites, 136–37, 139
Colonel Sanders, 54–55
commitment
    change and, 181, 182, 184–85, 187
    ideal station and, 247
    Lund Dental Practice and, 205, 206
    in start-ups, 211
    in turnarounds, 228–29, 232
contractor success, 214–21
contractors as businesses, 133–35
control, sense of, 17, 78, 79, 81, 144, 172
costs, watching, 245–46
Courtesy System
    in action, 202, 203
    children and, 205
    rules of, 206–8
    values and, 60, 193, 206
creative problem solving, 111–13, 174–75, 185–87
Crown, Henry, 14
cultural structures, xxiii–xxiv
    attributes of, 24, 25f, 27–28, 52
    building, 27–28
    changing, 23
    dysfunctional systems, 129
    feedback and, 96
    goals and, 64–65
    motivation and, 32, 35–36
cultural systems, 22, 24–29, 25f
culture
    adapting to, xxi–xxiii, 205, 252
    in transition, 223–40
customer appreciation, 85–88
"Customer Cancer", 16, 17, 18, 19, 23, 28
customer complaints, 124–25
customer culture, 18
customer experience goals, 65–66

customer feedback, 128
customer focus, 16, 18, 23, 152–55, 158–60, 238
customer goals, 64–67, 69, 71, 128, 237
customer interactions, 18
customer loyalty, 18–19
customer referrals, 66, 69, 204
customer service
    angry customers, 144–45
    employees and, 18, 67, 110, 169–70
    extraordinary service, 109–20
    Federal Express and, 142, 165–66
    feedback and, 112–15, 128, 169
    inventing service concepts, 111–13, 116
    stories about, 88–93
customer value, 17, 57
customer value-added chart, 42f
CustomerCulture, xxii, xxiv, 2, 16
    accountability, 238
    actions, 119, 238
    application of, 121–87, 209–21
    change and, 187
    feedback, 110, 119, 238
    goals, 93, 110, 119, 237
    implementing programs, 138
    relevance of goals, 93, 110, 119, 237–38
    results of, 189–240, 189–240
    in start-ups, 209–21
    theory of, 1–120
    turnarounds and, 224, 226
    values, 52, 92, 110, 119, 237
    vision, 52, 92, 110, 119, 237
customers
    control over destiny, 144
    focusing on, 154–55, 238
    quality of, 66–67
    quantity of, 66–67
    solving problems for, 141

D

dashboard, 128
deliverables, 25

Demand Marketing, 135–36
determination, 24
"Determined Men", 252, 258–65
diagnostic sessions, 230–33, 238
Done Services
    emotional needs and, 44–45, 48
    informational needs and, 46
    spiritual needs and, 51
dysfunctional cultural systems, 129

E

EAGLE cards, 85–88, 86f, 92
effectiveness, improving, xxiii–xxiv
egg analogy, 152
emotional dynamics, 233
emotional needs, 42f, 45, 47–50
employee goals, 64, 67–69, 71, 237
employees
    accountability, 248
    action of, 164–65
    challenging, 146, 150
    control over destiny, 17, 172
    customer loyalty, 18–19
    customer service, 67, 110, 169–70
    demanding best from, 18
    empowering, 85, 240
    happiness of, 67
    incentives, 74, 81, 124
    involving, 146
    loyalty of, 13
    mistakes, 247–48
    motivating, 32, 35–36, 74, 81, 124
    as problem solvers, 111–19, 146–
        47, 150
    raises for, 17
    value and, 52
empowerment, 85, 240
enjoyment of work, 85
EvianAir, 218, 220
excellence in products, 57
excellence in service, 57
extraordinary service, 109–20

F

facilitator, role of, 168–69, 231, 232
Fagan, Vince, 146
failure, and feedback, 12–13
fair dealings, 57
Federal Express, xxiv
    accountability, 248
    airline for, 4–5
    building, 243
    commitment, 247
    control over destiny, 79
    costs, 245–46
    creating FedEx Services, 157
    customer focus, 16, 23
    customer goals, 65–66
    customer service, 88, 90–92, 142,
        157
    emotional needs and, 48
    employee goals, 68
    employee mistakes, 247–48
    feedback for, 164
    feedback system, 96f, 96–97
    get-the-packages campaign, 6–13,
        15, 80, 96–97
    goals for, 162–64
    growth of, 158–59
    Guarantee of Fair Treatment, 60,
        79, 80–81
    healthcare system and, 105
    Hierarchy of Horrors and, 162–63
    ideal station, 242–49
    informational needs and, 45–47
    initial idea of, 177–80
    innovation of, 176
    interfaces, 247–48
    Leadership Index, 68, 69
    No Layoff policy, 79, 80, 145
    on-time delivery percentage, 162–
        63
    organizational structure, 152
    owner goals, 68–69
    people, 243–44
    People, Service, Profit values, 60–
        61, 69, 243
    perfection, 243, 246
    physical needs and, 45

PowerShip system, 145
problem solving, 36–38, 182–87
profitability goals, 244–45
rewarding actions, 83
separate operations and, 156–57
service goals, 244–45
Service Quality Index, 65–66, 69,
    163–64
spiritual needs and, 51
story of, 6–19
trust, 247
values of, 60–61
vision for, 242
weekly feedback report, 97–103,
    98f
workplace cleanliness, 247
FedEx Services, 157
feedback
    action and, xxiii, 13, 24–28, 97–
        103
    cultural structures and, 96
    from customers, 110, 112–15, 128,
        169, 210–11
    failure and, 12–13
    Federal Express and, 164
    goals and, 64–65
    importance of, 107
    loss of, 103–5
    Lund Dental Practice and, 106,
        193, 204
    programs and, 124–30
    results and, 24–28, 81–82
    in start-ups, 214, 218, 221
    system of, 96f, 96–103, 115, 117
    in turnarounds, 232
    weekly report, 97–98, 98f, 128
focus
    changing, 243
    on customers, 16, 18, 23, 152–55,
        158–60, 238
    on success, 128–30, 139
follow-up systems, 81–82
Frock, Roger, 96

G

General Dynamics, 14
General Motors, 149
Gerber, Michael, 135
Ghandi, 229
goals
    attributes of, 64–65
    balancing, 128–29
    categories of, 65–71
    for customers, 64–67, 69, 71, 169
    for employees, 64, 67–69, 71
    of Federal Express, 164
    focus on, 63–71
    of Lund Dental Practice, 193
    of manufacturing company, 127
    measuring, 64–65
    of new programs, 124–30
    number of, 65
    for owners, 64, 68–69, 71
    purpose of, 64
    recognizing goals, 83–85
    relevance of, xxiii, 13, 24–28, 30,
        35–36, 38, 64, 73–93,
        106, 110, 128, 164
    in start-ups, 212, 214, 221
    types of, 65
growth, 126–30, 153, 158–60
Guarantee of Fair Treatment (GFT), 60,
    79, 80–81

H

happiness-centered business, 193, 202,
    203, 206–8
Happiness Index, 204
Harley-Davidson, 50
Harley Owners' Group (HOG), 50
healthcare system
    loss of feedback, 103–5
    relevance of goals, 106
    systemic issues, 104–5
Hershey's Chocolate Company, 117–19
hierarchical organization, 152
Hierarchy of Horrors, 44, 85, 161–70
    benefits of, 170
    facilitators for, 168–69

Federal Express and, 162–63
identifying horrors, 162, 167–69, 194
HomeScan Business System, 219
honest dealings, 57
Hublein, 54
humanizing the exception, 145–50

I

IBM, 142–43
ideal station, 242–49
incentives, 74, 81, 124
indifference, of corporate leaders, 16
informational needs, 42f, 44–47
innovation in action, 209–21
innovative success, 181
integrity, 228, 229, 234, 237
interfaces, 247–48
inventing new systems, 118–19
inventing service concepts, 111–13, 116

J

Judd, Sandra, 111, 112

K

Kentucky Fried Chicken, 54–55

L

Larson-Juhl, xxiv–xxv
organizational structure, 152, 158–59
quality and, 59–60
rewarding actions, 83
values of, 57–58
leadership
by example, 57
role of, 224, 227, 230, 235–39
success and, 68, 69
Leadership Index, 68, 69
Lindenfelser, Walt, 90
listening skills, 85, 231–33

Lund Dental Practice, xxv
clients, 197–98
Courtesy System, 60, 193, 202, 203, 205–8
customer-friendly environment, 166–68
customer goals, 66–67
customer quality, 66–67
customer referrals, 66, 69, 204
emotional needs and, 47, 49–50
employee goals, 68
employee happiness, 69
feedback system, 106, 193, 204
goals, 69–70, 193
happiness-centered business, 193
Happiness Index, 204
informational needs and, 46–47
organizational culture, 152
physical needs and, 44, 45
problem solving, 194–96
profitability goals, 203–4
Referral Index, 66, 69, 204
revenue production, 70
spiritual needs and, 51–52
story of, 191–208
values of, 60
Lund, Paddi, xxv
on emotional needs, 46–47, 49
feedback system, 106
on goals, 67
identifying horrors, 166–67, 169
on physical needs, 45
story of, 191–208
on values, 60

M

Maguire, Frank, 54
manufacturing company
approach of, 132–34
goals of, 127
vision of, 126
market shares, 129
marketing programs, 135–36, 139, 214
McDonald's, 23
Microsoft, 143

motivation, 32, 35–36, 74, 81, 124

N

negative relevance system, 79
new programs, 124–30
No Layoff policy, 79, 80, 145
Nordstrom, 88

O

objective goals, 65
offers, testing, 136
organizational culture, xxi–xxii
organizational structures
    CEO on top, 152, 152f
    customers on top, 153, 154f
owner goals, 64, 68–69, 71, 237

P

partnerships, 132–34, 138–39, 214–21
Pay System, 76–77
People, Service, Profit values, 60–61,
    69, 243
People–Profit ethic, 9
perfection, 243, 246
performance
    appreciation and, 234–35
    cultural structures and, xxi, xxiv
    improving, 30–32
    rewards and, 57
personal needs. *See* emotional needs
personal values, 56
Peters, Tom, 176
Phoenix Dog Piss Theory, 123–30
physical needs, 42f, 43–45
policies, setting, 26
policy manuals, 239
positive behavior, recognizing, 83–85,
    92
Potential Improvement Point (PIP),
    231, 233, 238
PowerShip system, 145
price changes, 126
pricing structures, 67

problem resolution, 18
problem solving
    change and, 182–87
    employees and, 111–19, 174–75
    Federal Express and, 36–38
    Lund Dental Practice and, 194–96
    in start-ups, 215–16
problems, causes of, 30–34, 37–39
product excellence, 57
products, testing, 136
profitability goals
    Bell Sports and, 159
    Federal Express and, 158, 245
    growth and, 67, 126, 129, 130, 153,
        160
    Lund Dental Practice and, 203–4
    turnarounds and, 237
    UPS and, 70
programs, new, 124–25
programs, old, 124–25, 127
promises, giving, 85

Q

quality
    conveying, 48, 55, 200–201
    Larson-Juhl and, 59–60
    Lund Dental Practice and, 200–201
Quantum Growth Seminar, 219
quarterly goals, 127–28

R

Railway Express Agency (REA), 13
Referral Index, 66, 69, 204
regimes, replacing, 124–25
reinventing service, 111–13, 116
relevance of goals, xxiii, 73–93
    control and, 78, 79, 81
    customer appreciation, 85–88
    Federal Express and, 79–81
    feedback and, 13, 24–28, 64, 81–
        82, 110
    follow-up systems, 81–82
    healthcare systems, 106
    lack of, 29–30

motivation, 35–36, 38
negative systems, 79
new programs and, 124–30
Pay System™ and, 76–77
performance and, 81
recognizing goals, 83–85, 92
rewarding actions, 83
turnarounds and, 237–38
UPS and, 29–30, 35–36, 70, 74–77
respect, 57, 234–35
responsibility, acceptance of, 85, 248
revenue goals, 70
rewards, 57, 83
Roadway Package Service (RPS), 156

S

sales goals, 65, 67, 129
Sanders, Colonel, 54–55
security systems, 148
service culture, 15
service excellence, 57
service goals, 70, 244–45
Service Quality Index (SQI), 65–66, 69, 163–64
services, testing, 136
"Single Egg" organizations, 151–60, 155f, 238
Smith, Fred
95% rule and, 162
on control over destiny, 17, 78
Federal Express and, 4, 13, 14, 177–80
Hierarchy of Horrors and, 162–63
innovation of, 176
on leadership, 68
on people-centered companies, 71
on problem solving, 147
spiritual needs, 42f, 50–52
start-up, anatomy of, 209–21
subjective goals, 65
success indicator, 100–101
success, ingredients of, 181
sustainability, 126, 129–30, 153, 158, 160
Synectics, 146

systemizing the routine, 145–50
systems driving organizations, 22
systems driving people, 21–40
systems, inventing, 118–19

T

tech support service, 143
testing offers, 136
third-party companies, 132
top-line goals, 67, 129
trust, 224, 225, 227–29, 233–34, 237, 247
turnaround, anatomy of, 223–40
CEOs, 229–30
company problems, 226–27, 229–30
customer focus, 238
diagnostic process, 230–33, 238
emotional dynamics, 233
employee honesty, 227
trust, 224

U

Umile, Mario, 35
United Airlines, 13
United Parcel Service. See UPS
United States Postal Service (USPS), 17
UPS (United Parcel Service), xxiv–xxv
cost-reduction goal, 29, 30–32
cultural structures, 28–32
customer focus, 23
customer service stories, 89–90
determination of, 29
emotional needs and, 48
incentives, 74
labor disputes, 71
motivation, 35–36, 38, 74
owner goals, 70
performance-improving system, 30–32
philosophy of, 251–65
problem to resolve, 28–33, 35–36
profitability goals, 70

relevance of goals, 29–30, 35–36, 70, 74–77
service goals, 70
spiritual needs and, 51
values of, 56–57
vision, 29, 253
urgency, sense of, 18

V

value. *See also* values
of cleanliness, 47, 48, 55, 247
of customers, 57
perception of, 42–43
value curve, 42f, 44, 46, 52
Value Violation, 56, 57, 237
values, 53–61
awards for, 58
boundaries for, 25, 54
chart of, 42f
defining corporations, 54
of Federal Express, 60–61
of Larson-Juhl, 57–58
living, 56

of Lund Dental Practice, 60
setting, 26
in start-ups, 211, 218
of UPS, 56–57
vision and, 24–28, 61, 110
vision, 41–52
description of, 52
for Federal Express, 242
of manufacturing company, 126–27
purpose of, 242
setting, 26
in start-ups, 211, 215, 218–19, 221
values and, 24–28, 61, 110

W

Wal-Mart, 23
Web site development, 136–37
weekly feedback report, 97–103, 98f, 128
work, enjoying, 85
workplace cleanliness, 247

8 reasons why you should read the Financial Times for 4 weeks RISK-FREE!

To help you stay current with significant
developments in the world economy ...
and to assist you to make informed business
decisions — the Financial Times brings you:

① Fast, meaningful overviews of international affairs ... plus daily
briefings on major world news.

② Perceptive coverage of economic, business, financial and political
developments with special focus on emerging markets.

③ More international business news than any other publication.

④ Sophisticated financial analysis and commentary on world market
activity plus stock quotes from over 30 countries.

⑤ Reports on international companies and a section on global investing.

⑥ Specialized pages on management, marketing, advertising and
technological innovations from all parts of the world.

⑦ Highly valued single-topic special reports (over 200 annually)
on countries, industries, investment opportunities, technology and more.

⑧ The Saturday Weekend FT section — a globetrotter's guide to
leisure-time activities around the world: the arts, fine dining, travel,
sports and more.

FT FINANCIAL TIMES
World business newspaper

The *Financial Times* delivers a world of business news.

Use the Risk-Free Trial Voucher below!

To stay ahead in today's business world you need to be well-informed on a daily basis. And not just on the national level. You need a news source that closely monitors the entire world of business, and then delivers it in a concise, quick-read format.

With the *Financial Times* you get the major stories from every region of the world. Reports found nowhere else. You get business, management, politics, economics, technology and more.

Now you can try the *Financial Times* for 4 weeks, absolutely risk free. And better yet, if you wish to continue receiving the *Financial Times* you'll get great savings off the regular subscription rate. Just use the voucher below.

Where to find tomorrow's best business and technology ideas. TODAY.

- Ideas for defining tomorrow's competitive strategies — and executing them.

- Ideas that reflect a profound understanding of today's global business realities.

- Ideas that will help you achieve unprecedented customer and enterprise value.

- Ideas that illuminate the powerful new connections between business and technology.

ONE PUBLISHER.

Financial Times Prentice Hall.

FINANCIAL TIMES
Prentice Hall

WORLD BUSINESS PUBLISHER

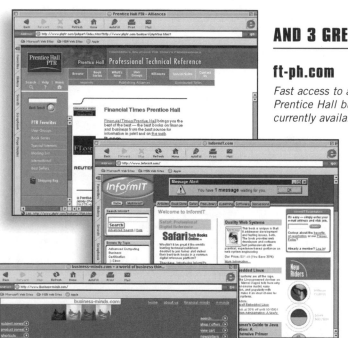

AND 3 GREAT WEB SITES:

ft-ph.com

Fast access to all Financial Times Prentice Hall business books currently available.

InformIt.com

Your link to today's top business and technology experts: new content, practical solutions, and the world's best online training.

Business-minds.com

Where the thought leaders of the business world gather to share key ideas, techniques, resources — and inspiration.